2 WEEK LOAN

This item is to be returned to the library on or before the last date stamped below.

Leeds City College

BE ☐ EN ☐ HF ☐ PL ☐ PW ☒ TC ☐

Renew on 0113

216 2046   or   284 6246   or   386 1705

www.lcc-library.appspot.com

KoganPage

LONDON PHILADELPHIA NEW DELHI

D0177328

First published in Great Britain and the United States in 2012 by Kogan Page Limited

120 Pentonville Road
London N1 9JN
United Kingdom
www.koganpage.com

1518 Walnut Street, Suite 1100
Philadelphia PA 19102
USA

4737/23 Ansari Road
Daryaganj
New Delhi 110002
India

© Warren Redman, 2012

ISBN   978 0 7494 6556 8
E-ISBN 978 0 7494 6557 5

British Library Cataloguing-in-Publication Data

A CIP record for this book is available from the British Library.

Library of Congress Cataloging-in-Publication Data

Redman, Warren.
    Emotional fitness coaching : how to develop a positive and productive workplace for leaders, managers and coaches / Warren Redman.
        p. cm.
    Includes bibliographical references.
    ISBN 978-0-7494-6556-8 – ISBN 978-0-7494-6557-5   1. Executive coaching.   2. Leadership.
3. Emotional intelligence.   4. Work environment.   I. Title.
    HD30.4.R423 2012
    658.4'07124–dc23
                                                                                              2011052735

Typeset by Graphicraft Ltd, Hong Kong
Printed and bound in India by Replika Press Pvt Ltd

CONTENTS

Introduction
Developing healthy and productive workplace practices for managers, mentors and coaches

The world of work has, up until very recently, been seen as a world in which the dominant and most valued skills are mental and physical. They are the 'hard skills' of thinking and fixing, buying and selling, talking and making. Today, there are a growing awareness and understanding that our emotional skills are what make the difference between success and mediocrity. These are the 'soft skills'. Here's the problem. The soft skills are really the hard ones.

The development of coaching as a recognized profession and skill set has largely been an acknowledgement that it is difficult, without help, to deal with the things that block us from making progress, or leave us feeling frustrated and stuck, or unclear how to handle conflict or anger.

Emotional Fitness Coaching offers a unique set of tools designed for managers who desire to hone their coaching and mentoring skills, or for coaches who work externally, wishing to do the same. The tools described in this book have been developed over a period of thirty years. The criteria for including them here are that they work, that they are simple, and that above all they all acknowledge the individual's ability to make their own best choices and be accountable for them.

Five E-Fitness coaching tools are described. The first is Power Listening, in which you will discover the two things that prevent effective listening from taking place and the five stages of listening that make it work. The second is Learning from Experience, describing a system that encourages staff at all levels to consider and learn from what goes on in the organization. The third is the Group Dialogue; a method of running meetings that transforms them from time-wasting and costly sessions into creative opportunities for significant change. The fourth is the Workscale, a questionnaire like no other that allows people to see their levels of satisfaction and frustration, and provides them with the tools to make the desired changes. The fifth and final tool described here is Storytelling. The telling of stories in E-Fitness coaching is a refreshing and creative way for people to discover important things about the way they see things, including themselves and each other.

All of the tools, used in the hands of a competent E-Fitness coach, or manager who develops the skills, will improve communication, raise people's level of motivation and loyalty, decrease stress, along with absenteeism and errors, and have a significant impact on the productivity, health and eventual profitability of any company.

In line with its subject, and one of the tools in particular, the book is written as a story, and as an invitation for you to take part.

Adam is a newly appointed manager, with an unexpected and very quick promotion on the near horizon. He meets by chance the person who becomes his E-Fitness coach. Each chapter introduces another tool in the E-Fitness toolkit, and in each episode, Adam tries it out in the company he works for. He listens to his boss and he even tries out Power Listening at home. Most important of all, he starts to listen to himself and makes some startling and very positive discoveries.

His coach demonstrates to Adam the cost and even disasters that can occur when people and organizations fail to learn from their experiences, and shows a simple method, which Adam practises at work. He takes on the challenge of trying it out with a senior manager who has a negative outlook and who has excellent practical skills but little leadership expertise.

While most coaching focuses on the individual, the reality is that many managers work with teams and, like it or not, hold meetings. Adam is in charge of a team of regional sales managers and, with the help of his coach, runs a meeting that creates a new sense of energy and enthusiasm.

Each of the five tools is experienced fully by Adam, and each is tried out by him at work. The Workscale brings him to a clearer understanding of his purpose and his fears and how to overcome them. He then uses the Workscale with two other managers. The same happens with Storytelling, except that Adam tries it out within a sales training event, finding it to be a highly effective team development tool.

The remaining chapters deal with how you, sometimes with Adam leading the way, can bring E-Fitness coaching into your workplace, helping you define your goals, create a winning business case and implement the steps for success.

If the results are half as extraordinary for you as they have been for me, you will be amazed. The simplicity and power of coaching using these Emotional Fitness methods can only be appreciated once they are experienced. Enjoy the experience.

Why Emotional Fitness brings success

01

The encounter

Adam rose early. He hadn't slept well and by the time the kids burst into the bedroom at just before six he was already downstairs with a cup of coffee in one hand and a copy of the sales report in the other. When Adam whispered that he was going to take a walk to clear his mind before taking the train, Pauline had sleepily said she would handle the two boisterous beings this morning. In the past couple of weeks they had talked at length about this very day. He still didn't feel ready. No matter what he read about management and leadership, no matter the number of times he attended courses, he still had a sense of doom. Only Pauline knew about this. The smiling ebullience he portrayed at work had effectively, far too effectively it now seemed, brought him to the next stepping stone to the success he desired.

A cool early spring morning greeted him as he left the house and, turning left at the corner, made his way to the park. This route added another 15 minutes to his walk, but was one that he enjoyed and tried to take once in a while. It gave him some thinking time. He could even take in some of the sights, sounds and scents that the park offered up. This morning he had given himself sufficient time to absorb something of nature. His train didn't leave for nearly an hour.

He entered the park by the south gate and instead of taking the path leading diagonally across towards the east gate, which was his shortest route to the High Street and thence to the station, he followed the path northwards to the middle of the park. Here stood the centrepiece, the pride and joy of the town: a fountain and statue reminiscent of those to be found all over Italy but so rare in this, or indeed any, part of England. Benches circled the fountain. Adam headed for one of them, when he noticed a figure approaching the same bench from the west side. It was a tall man, with a slight stoop and an unmistakable gait. Adam's first instinct was to leave the path, walk across the grass and head to the other side of the fountain. Too late. The man had seen him. The man waved at him. 'This,' Adam thought, 'cannot be happening today.'

Adam knew that his old boss, Keith Parkinson, lived somewhere in the vicinity, but he had never seen him in the park until now.

Forty minutes later, Adam hurried out of the park to catch his train. His head was spinning and his spirit soared. This day, this new job, was something he now looked forward to. He opened his laptop on the train and wrote down everything that he had just learned. He wished he'd had an audio recorder to capture the conversation. How had it started?

'I'm well, thank you, Adam,' was Keith's rejoinder to the only question Adam could think of asking to start a conversation. And then Keith said, 'Tell me how you are doing.'

That was the first thing Adam noted down. Keith had begun with a request for information that was not a question. It was more than a question; it was an invitation. Before he knew it, Adam was spilling out the news of his promotion, his new boss, the challenges he faced and, to his own surprise, the trepidation he felt at taking on a management role. The irony was palpable. Here he was, sitting on a park bench talking to the man who had been his boss in that very role two years ago and whom Adam had despised for his inability to lead effectively. Even more ironically, he was talking to a man who had never listened to him before and was now apparently able to take in every word Adam was saying.

Anxious that he might forget some of the gems from their conversation, Adam resorted to making a list, adding brief notes and questions. He planned to see Keith again and wanted to be prepared this time. He reviewed what he had written.

1 Employee well-being and organizational performance are inextricably linked. (How?)

2 Emotional health is the core of well-being. (What does that mean?)

3 Leadership skills in the 21st century must focus on the emotional health of employees.

4 The ability to listen proactively is the most valuable of those skills. (How did Keith learn that? Why didn't he know it when he was my boss?)

5 There is more real and perceived value when providing opportunities to learn from what goes on in the organization than from training. (How do we do that?)

6 Meetings can be transformational, both for the team members and the company. (Can't wait to see that.)

7 When individuals and organizations have a good energy balance, they function well. When they are not balanced, they are dysfunctional. (?)

8 Storytelling can inspire employees to bring out their best. (In our company?)

9 Good managers use coaching with their employees. Great managers use Emotional Fitness coaching. (What happened to Keith? Where was he when I needed him?)

Adam snapped shut the laptop just as the train arrived at its destination. Now he would see if anything stuck to him today.

The entry

'Good morning, Adam. Or should I call you Sir now? How's our new regional sales manager?'

Adam smiled wanly at the receptionist. 'Thanks, Claudia, Adam it still is. And I'm doing great. Is Evelyn in?'

Evelyn greeted him warmly as he stepped into her office, closing the door behind him. She had been in the new position of sales director for six months, since when things had changed quite a bit. Adam was part of the change. As he sat across the desk from his new boss, Adam was conscious of the dampness in his hands and under his armpits. His toes curled in his shoes. Evelyn was speaking. Suddenly he remembered Keith. Something switched in his brain. He leaned forward slightly, paying her full attention.

The meeting lasted no more than 15 minutes, after which he walked down the corridor to his new office only two doors from Evelyn's, which he would be sharing with two other regional sales managers. The difference was that, since the company's HQ was also in his region, Adam would have the space to himself much of the time. Matthew, the maintenance man, arrived just as Adam did, holding in his hand the nameplate, which he proceeded to screw onto the door over the blank space that had previously held the name of his predecessor, Patrick Strong. Adam had felt the discomfort of being promoted to replace a man who effectively had been fired for, he mused, not being strong enough.

It was still early; not time enough for the calls to come in and the expected demands of his new job to begin kicking in. No doubt there was a backlog, but another hour wouldn't make much of a difference. Adam reflected on his morning so far.

He had listened to Evelyn; and he realized he had listened to himself as well; at least paid enough attention to what was going on for him to relax and concentrate on Evelyn instead of his own fears. The result was that he had seen Evelyn not just as the director brought in to shake up the sales force; not just the MBA with a highly successful sales and marketing career behind her; not only the niece of the company's boss and co-founder Marcus Baines; and not simply as an ambitious, hard-nosed executive. He had seen her as human. Underneath the clipped, concise tone and the businesslike way in which she outlined the major points within the overall sales targets and what she expected from his region, he detected the human face that he had missed before. He had observed concern in her eyes and in the way she hesitated and dropped her voice, only for a brief moment, before she wished him good luck. He didn't know what to make of the concern. Was it concern for him, for the sales targets, for her choice in picking him for this job? He couldn't know, nor was he going to ask. All that had happened was that he felt a little different. The pressure was still there, but he no longer felt that it was only his. In a strange way, he believed he had discovered a partner. Rather than Evelyn being the one who put the pressure on him, it now seemed that they shared that same sense of pressure. He had no idea what to do with this.

The phone started to ring.

First things first

The Corner Café was the ideal place for this. Adam settled himself and his cup of coffee behind the small circular table, close to the window. He was five minutes early. Few people were around at this time of the morning. He had hardly brought the cup to his lips when he saw the unmistakable loping stride of Keith crossing the road towards the café. Adam had his questions, and more that had emerged over the past week, but he really wanted to know what he and Keith would be doing. After their chance conversation in the park, Adam's initial enthusiasm for what Keith had said seemed to have dwindled in the face of a mountain of work. He had taken up Keith's invitation to call him and pursue that conversation with a view to taking it further and helping him in his new job. Now Adam wondered whether he wasn't in danger of overloading himself with ideas that could never be implemented.

Following the initial pleasantries, they got down to business.

'First thing,' said Keith, 'I'd like to know what you are really looking for from this conversation, and I will tell you what I can and can't offer. Before even that, I want to let you know that anything you talk about is strictly between us. I won't share anything you say with anyone else, certainly not without your full agreement. The other thing is that I am not going to let the fact that I was your boss in a previous life get in the way of any of our discussions. We can talk more about those things. But first, as I said, tell me what you want from our conversation.'

Adam pondered for a moment. He wasn't sure what he wanted apart from having his inquisitiveness satisfied. 'I have a few questions,' he began. 'Actually I wrote them down. Some of them are about you.'

'That's good,' said Keith. 'Let's begin with those questions.'

Adam went through his notes. 'You mentioned the link between employee well-being and company performance, then you said that well-being was really about emotional health. You also said that leaders have to focus on the emotional health of their employees, and then you said that listening was the most valuable skill. Can you tell me more about that? And while you're at it, I hope you don't mind me asking, but I'd like to know how you got to know those things. How did you get so good at listening when, if you'll forgive me, I didn't notice that when you were my boss at Baines?'

'I don't mind at all, Adam, and you certainly don't need to be forgiven for being open. Those are really good questions, and since you have them all written down already, we won't forget them. I want to address all of them with you. Anything else?'

'Yes,' said Adam. 'You talked about learning being better than training and I wondered how we do that. You also talked about meetings being transformational and after this week I'd like even more to know how that can be done. You brought up balance and although I think I know what you mean I'd like to hear your take on it. I kind of squirmed when you mentioned storytelling. I think it scared me, so there is a question around that. Finally, you used the term Emotional Fitness when you said that great managers use Emotional Fitness coaching. I want to know about that. Is that enough?'

'It's enough to start with. We have begun to form a contract with one another. I fancy another coffee. Would you like one? Then I'd like to begin with the last question first, which will lead into all the others. How does that sound?'

After they settled back into their chairs, fresh cups of coffee in front of them, Keith began speaking.

'I noticed that when I said the word "contract", you looked a little startled, so I want to explain what I mean. If we are to do anything together, I intend that it is quite clear between us what each of us expects. That's why I asked you to tell me what you want. I'm sure there is more and we will come to that. As far as I'm concerned, apart from offering you the confidentiality that I mentioned earlier, I would like to offer you my services as a coach – and more specifically, as an Emotional Fitness coach. We can call it E-Fitness for short. And before you get the wrong idea, I am not charging you for my services. As a matter of fact, you will be assisting me at the same time. You see, I have just completed an intensive training as an E-Fitness coach and part of the final requirement is that I coach three people over a period of time. The only stipulation is that the person I coach agrees to provide my trainer with an evaluation of the process and of my competencies as an E-Fitness coach. My own feedback to my trainer will be about the processes I use, not what you talk about. I would like to offer you 10 sessions to go through these processes and at all times focus on what it is that you bring to the table; so your questions are what we will attend to first. How does that sound so far?'

Adam looked at Keith. This wasn't at all the man he remembered as his boss. Then he was unclear, distracted, unfocused and sometimes dismissive. He was the one whom Adam had tried to avoid in the park. Now Adam felt drawn to him. Could there really have been such a change?

'I'll give it a go,' he said. 'I am very grateful for the offer and I'll do my bit. Actually it couldn't have come at a better time for me.'

The overview

'This coaching,' said Keith, 'is going to be mostly you talking and me listening. This first bit is going to be a little different, because you have those questions and because you want to know something about how I have come to learn about E-Fitness. In other words, this first session or two will be more me talking so that you can understand the context of this approach and how it applies to you and your work. The other sessions will focus on what you want to achieve for your own personal and professional development and therefore you will be doing the talking. My job will be to assist you to draw out your own wisdom, not to give you advice.'

'Hmm,' murmured Adam, 'assuming I have wisdom, it would be nice to draw it out. But I don't quite see what wisdom has to do with Emotional Fitness.'

Keith smiled. 'Thanks for the lead-in. Let me tell you about my own journey and discoveries since I left Baines; only because it will help to make clearer what I want you to know.

'I worked for the company for 22 years; for the first 12 years as a sales representative and the last ten as regional sales manager when they first established the role after the reorganization of the sales side. Marcus Baines realized he couldn't do it all himself. I was good at sales, and when I was promoted it was a challenge but also fun to develop a sales team of my own. Then things began to change. The sales team were such a varied lot. I began to get pressure from them, pressure from the manufacturing supervisor, pressure from Mr Baines, who would look at me sadly, and just pressure from the pile on my desk. To cap it all, my wife became ill and I was really worried about her. Luckily I have three wonderful children, young adults actually, who pitched in; but I was getting really stressed out. Frankly,

I was falling to pieces. I certainly wasn't enjoying work any more, and it showed in my performance and in the performance of the whole sales team. In the end I decided that staying on didn't do me, the company or my family any good. Fortunately, I had enough savings, plus a small, but big enough, inheritance to allow me to think about early retirement. Most people in that position can't even consider it these days. I was 55 years old. That was two years ago, as you know. They gave Patrick Strong my job, which I thought was a mistake. I really fancied you for it, except they probably thought you were a bit young and inexperienced at the time.'

The café was filling up and the conversation around them brought their heads a little closer together.

'Anyway,' continued Keith, 'I spent the first year of my retirement with my family. We took a vacation: the first time for years we had all been away together. I played a lot of golf. I painted the house and fixed things that had been coming apart for ages. My wife's health improved. The kids moved on. I got bored. What was I going to do for the rest of my life? I started reading stuff – you know, books on personal development, mentoring and coaching, things like that. It was fascinating and I started to wonder what it would have been like if I'd known all of that when I was working. When I read a book on Emotional Fitness I began to put it together.

'Here's some of what I learned. Of all the qualities that contribute to being a successful person, or organization, the one that stands out is his, her or its level of Emotional Fitness. It took some time before I could absorb that, so I don't expect you to take it at face value immediately or without further exploration. Success, after all, is a subjective term and depends on whom you ask. At least that's so for an individual. Financial achievement, or at least a person's wealth, is measurable and might mean success. Of course, status has a very significant bearing on whether one feels successful or not. Where you live and what you do and how high up on the ladder you are at work may all mean success. But what I discovered, the more people I asked, the more I read and the more I thought about myself, was that success is just about how I feel. If, at this moment, I feel a sense of inner balance no matter what is going on around me, that I am at peace with myself, perhaps excited about possibilities and ready to take on whatever is in front of me, what better success could I have? The even greater insight came when I understood that in that state, the state of feeling good about myself, I was more positive about what I did and I was actually more productive and the results were better. I proved that to myself when I painted the house and when I had conversations with my family. The quality of everything went up in direct proportion to my feeling good. It had an impact on others too.'

'I can see that,' said Adam. 'And what about organizations? How do they exhibit Emotional Fitness? Surely success for Baines Electronics is measured by how much profit it makes.'

'Of course, that's true for all businesses. I asked myself two questions there. One was: does it help the bottom line for a business to be emotionally fit? The second was: is success to be measured purely by a company's profit? I couldn't really answer the first question; I didn't have enough evidence. Now I believe there are enough examples to show that it not only helps, but that a company can be turned around when E-Fitness is applied. The other question about whether profits are enough is answered simply by looking around and asking some more questions. Are the employees happy? Are the customers happy? We can usually measure those things indirectly.'

'Like, do employees stay or is staff turnover a problem?' Adam was animated. 'I know how expensive it is to recruit and train new people for any kind of job, and it's also costly to have people stick around when they are really no good at what they do. Like Patrick Strong, come to think of it.'

Keith looked at him intently. 'And just in case you were thinking this: like me too in my last five or so years on the job.' He moved on, saving Adam the dilemma of how to respond. 'The point is that at the very least, there is a significant cost to any organization when people are unhappy in their work. In that I include those who feel stressed, those who lack self-confidence, don't feel properly rewarded, either financially or through acknowledgement, don't have an outlet for taking any initiative, have any sense of creativity dampened – and I could go on.'

'For example,' added Adam, 'staff who don't get a chance to voice their opinions in meetings or who are ignored if they do.'

'You have it,' replied Keith. 'In all of those cases, we can see that when people in organizations are not happy, they don't function well; and when people don't function well, the organization is not as successful as it could be. It's not rocket science. As a matter of fact, we've seen that where rocket scientists aren't happy in their work, rockets fail with disastrous consequences. Remember Challenger? Train accidents are a similar case in point. Remember the Clapham Junction disaster and the Hidden Report? Of course you don't; you were too young. Briefly, stress at work and pressure from the poor management that led to it resulted in people dying in both cases. No; we can't measure success just in terms of money. Yes?'

Keith had seen a question formulating itself. Adam's knitted brow hadn't quite reached the precise question, but Keith's invitation brought it out.

'I do see this. What I want to know is how to do anything about it. The other thing is; I know something about Emotional Intelligence. We had a training session on it and used some kind of assessment test. EQ-i I think it was called. I didn't come out too badly, although there were a couple of things I could improve on. But what I want to know is: what's the difference between that and what you're talking about? How do we, how can I, make a difference to people's happiness at work, or feeling of success, as you put it?'

'That's another terrific question, Adam. I see that it takes us to the next level. I also see what the time is and I know that you have to get going. How about this? We meet next week at the same time. Meanwhile, I'd like you to make a note of those things from what you've heard that you see as important and relevant. During the week observe opportunities for improvement in your work in the way people communicate and how things happen. In other words, come back next time ready to say what you would like to change in your work situation, especially in your own responses to what is going on.'

Impending change

Marcus Baines arrived, as usual, at the plant just before seven am. He let himself in through the security gate and into the warehouse, walking through it until he reached the door of the factory. Taking his time, he strolled past the various stations, peering at loops of wire, strands of copper, capacitors, cables, switches: all the stock-in-trade of his business, and reflected how much had changed since he and his brother Trevor started with an idea. Then, over 45 years ago, Trevor had been the brains and the inspiration. When his brother died tragically just two years later, Marcus had struggled to keep the business afloat. His learning curve was more of a dramatic spike. Now, and every morning when he walked through, his ritual demanded that he glance up at the photograph of the two brothers standing in front of their first factory – little more than a shed in their back garden. The ritual apart, this morning was different. For the first time in their marriage, his wife Beatrice had asked him the question he had been waiting for. 'When are you going to slow down? When are you going to retire, Marcus?'

He congratulated himself that he was ready with the answer. He had been preparing. The absence of children had offered no obvious successor. There was nobody in his employment to whom he cared to hand over the business. The solution had presented itself, or rather herself, six months ago. Since Evelyn had arrived on the scene Beatrice seemed to have restrained herself from asking the question, and with her immaculate sense of timing, his wife had now posed her question.

Who better than Trevor's daughter, Marcus's only niece, to take over Baines Electronics? She had just the credentials: an MBA, a 14-year career as sales director with a strong background in marketing, and ambition. So what if her job had been with a cosmetics company? She could learn as much about the electronics industry as she needed to know, just as Marcus had. When Evelyn parted from her company, it seemed too good an opportunity to miss. She had her doubts at first; the apparent chasm between cosmetics and electronics and from an almost totally female staff to a mainly male one, at least in the management and sales side, appeared to her too big to leap across. But Marcus was persuasive and, he had to admit to himself, so enthusiastic that it was catching. The job he offered was in the new position he wanted to establish as sales director. The real carrot was the promise of the business. The only problem was that he had thought and spoken in terms of five years. Perhaps he had to reconsider that. Might be more like months.

Marcus left the factory through the door leading directly to the office suites and stepped into his own spacious and comfortable office. Andrea, his personal assistant for the past 26 years, had already started the coffee. The two of them were always in the building first. Soon the place would be humming. This was his thinking time.

'Andrea,' he called through the adjoining door to her office. 'Could you ask Evelyn to drop in to see me when she gets in?'

How things go wrong

By the time Adam arrived at the office he had the notes of what he had learned from Keith in his laptop. He had his project; he was going to keep his eyes and ears and other senses open to what went on around him. He had also checked into the Clapham Junction and the Challenger disasters on his computer. He wanted to understand for himself how such things could happen and how they could be avoided by people being more emotionally fit.

Keith was wrong about one thing. Adam remembered both events. He was 15 when the train crash occurred and he had followed the news of the tragedy closely. As for Challenger, even though he was only 12 at the time, the imprint of the televised explosion was etched into his mind. Reading over the results of the enquiries that followed, he was struck by the similarities in the circumstances leading up to each catastrophe.

In the case of Clapham Junction, in which 35 people died and 500 were injured, the immediate cause was an incorrect and faulty piece of wiring left in place by an inexperienced and tired worker who was just finishing a very long shift. The larger cause of the accident went much deeper into the heart of the organization. According to the Hidden Report, so-called because it was chaired by Anthony Hidden QC, British Rail senior management failed to recognize that the resignalling of the Clapham Junction area should have been treated as a major, safety-critical project, controlled throughout by a single, senior, named project manager. Instead the job was left to middle-level technical staff, stressed, poorly supervised by their seniors and poorly supported by their juniors. Staffing levels were inadequate and the employees, dulled by months of heavy overtime, were carrying out the complete resignalling of the largest and busiest junction on the whole British rail system. [Source: Wikipedia]

The Space Shuttle Challenger's demise was caused by the failure of an 'O-ring'. Once again, a tiny piece of equipment had caused a major disaster. Once again, what contributed to that piece of equipment failing, according to the Rogers's Commission and subsequent reports, was human behaviour. While engineers had warned for years about the safety concerns they had about the O-rings, management at NASA were preoccupied with meeting their flight schedule, no doubt egged on by their political masters. Ethical procedures were stretched beyond breaking point. All seven crew members were killed.

Adam pondered the information, recalling that he had read it before and on at least one occasion had been exposed to the information during a training session. This time, he considered what might have happened if those responsible at all levels had exhibited more emotional fitness. Someone would have said, 'No; this is not right.' Someone would have recognized the stress that was being handed down and reviewed what was actually happening. Someone would have openly said what was important. Someone would have listened. Challenger might not have taken off for several months. The worst that would have happened would have been disappointment. Christa McAuliffe, destined to be the first teacher in space, would still be alive. The arrival of three commuter trains into Clapham Junction that Monday morning in December 1988 would have been uneventful.

Adam pondered on the recalls of manufactured goods that had been on the news lately: everything from cars and toys to drugs and processed food. He remembered the batch of faulty circuit boards that Baines had sent out two years ago. Most had gone to one of his own customers, who had called Adam to complain that they didn't work. It had been a small error, but it cost the company a lot of money and nearly the loss of a good customer. Mr Baines had been very upset but nothing really happened apart from the section supervisor getting his team to work 10 hours a day for a week to put things right. The whisper had been that the ineffective circuit boards had been due to a design fault. Adam knew that the designer and the section supervisor had previously been on bad terms, and that the designer had been away on stress leave for a while, although he didn't know why. Now he wondered how better leadership could inspire better relationships and improved communication. Surely the company would have saved money and its reputation for quality if somebody had been more emotionally fit.

The challenge

Evelyn Young closed the door to her office and sat behind her desk. She unclenched her jaw, eased her fingers open. Marcus was great as an uncle. Why hadn't she let it stay that way? She loved his unassuming, mentoring, encouraging style when she was his niece. She needed a boss who was much clearer, more direct and decisive. On the other hand, isn't that what she had from Serena, her former boss at the cosmetics firm who, in the end, she found to be far too controlling and manipulative?

The brief meeting with Marcus had changed things. Now he wanted her to take over the reins in about six months, not five years. At one level, this was exactly what she had wanted. The problem was his totally unrealistic expectations. He was living in a dream world. The sales targets and the expansion of the business were based on his picturesque imagination rather than the facts. Evelyn had spent the past six months examining the facts. Competition was intense; they could never keep up with the prices from Asia anyway, but now they were no longer at the cutting edge of design. Meanwhile confidence in the economy was such that even though sales overall for electronic equipment were still fairly buoyant, price points were crucial and customer loyalty less solid. And did Marcus have any idea how long it took to get a strong foothold in new markets overseas, which is where he envisaged making a breakthrough? Worst of all, his plans seemed to be based almost exclusively on his confidence in Evelyn. This could turn out to be a nightmare, not the dream opportunity she had imagined. She had to get the sales team really moving; she had to get ready to recruit and train new technical staff; she had to develop a different kind of attitude in the whole management and supervisory team. If she was going to become managing director, she would have to find a new sales director; or promote one of the regional sales managers. And she had to make sure that she didn't burn herself out again like she had in her previous job.

Pressure and stress

'This morning we will review what you have discovered and complete the conversation we started last time.' Keith wasted no time in getting down to it.

'It was quite a roller coaster of a week,' Adam began. 'I have some big news; but I want to start with what I learned from what I observed. The main thing I noticed was how easy it is to pass stress on to others, and then what can happen as a result. For example, and I know this is confidential so I feel okay talking about people, my boss was stressed about something that her boss, Marcus Baines, had said to her. She talked to me and proposed some big changes. I felt stressed. The next thing is I find myself shouting down the phone to one of my salespeople. A couple of hours later I call back to apologize and discover that he's left early to go home, complaining that he wasn't feeling well enough to concentrate on his calls.'

'Excellent example,' said Keith. 'In the work we'll do together, it's important that you distinguish between pressure and stress. There is always going to be pressure, it seems to be the nature of our industrious lives. In fact, pressure is probably a vital part of what motivates and often inspires us to perform better. It is our reaction to pressure that can bring about stress. In other words, pressure may be externally generated. Stress always comes from within. This means that, even if your boss feels stress and puts pressure on you as a result, you can choose whether or not to take it on as stress, or whether to accept the fact that here is another challenge. Do you want to tell me what the big news is? I have a feeling it may be connected.'

'You are so right.' Adam flushed. 'Evelyn asked me to consider taking on her job – becoming sales director in just six months. I've only just been made regional sales manager. I've hardly slept a wink since then. Pauline and I have talked about nothing else and I still don't know what to do. I wanted to wait until you and I spoke. One thing I did think is that if I do take this huge responsibility I want to be a really good leader and I want the kind of qualities that we talked about last time. When I shouted at Max the sales guy a few days ago, after coming away from meeting with Evelyn and feeling overwhelmed, I certainly wasn't emotionally fit.'

Adam paused, returning Keith's intense gaze. 'Frankly,' continued Adam, 'what I need is not so much the theory. I need the skills. I need to know how to be that leader who listens and makes sure that people learn from mistakes and how to run meetings that are really productive and those other things you talked about. But I suppose before I even go down that path I need to know why it's such a good idea. Does it really work?'

Keith took a sip of coffee, put the cup down carefully and put his fingers together.

EQ and E-Fitness: the difference

'That seems to take us to the point where we left off last week. I will talk more about E-Fitness and how it connects with but is also very distinct from Emotional Intelligence, since you asked that last time. I shall also try my best to answer your other questions. After that, if you want to go ahead, we can go through the practice of becoming a great leader coach using the tools of E-Fitness.'

Adam settled himself. He wanted to concentrate on what Keith would tell him now.

'We share the same interest in at least one important respect,' Keith continued. 'We both want to have some practical tools that work. Perhaps it's the electronics background that does it, but somehow I don't think so. I am less interested in the why of things than in the how of them. That's not to say that this work isn't based on a deep understanding of what makes people act in certain ways and what qualities are needed to improve their behaviour. Emotional Fitness has its roots in some of the great teachers and psychotherapists of the 20th century, although you may not have heard of them. Men like Carl Rogers, Eric Berne and Fritz Perls. Most significantly, it was the theory and practice of Human Social Functioning, created by Eugene Heimler in the 1960s and 1970s, that inspired the development of Emotional Fitness.

'Before the turn of this century, Emotional Intelligence started to make its mark, just at the same time that Emotional Fitness was being developed. The two came from totally different sources. The only similarity was in the use of the word 'emotional'. Few at the time wanted to touch the 'E' word – certainly in the workplace. Daniel Goleman made Emotional Intelligence popular with his book of that title in 1996. Goleman hadn't coined the term; it had been in circulation by psychologists for 30 years; but he certainly put it on the map, arguing that non-cognitive 'intelligence' was as important as, if not more important than, intellectual intelligence for people who wanted to be successful in any kind of leadership positions. He produced a set of five basic emotional competencies under the headings of self-awareness, self-regulation, motivation, empathy and social skills. Another psychologist, Reuven Bar-On, also developed a theory of emotional–social intelligence; with five similar factors that measured someone's emotional abilities. He calls the first intrapersonal, or self-awareness and self-expression, for example one's self-regard and level of assertiveness. The second is interpersonal, which is more to do with social awareness, such as having empathy. Third is stress management, or emotional management and control. The next is adaptability, which he also calls change management, such as the ability to problem solve. Finally there is what he describes as general mood, or self-motivation, such as having optimism. If you completed an EQ-i questionnaire, it was probably Bar-On's.'

'I think it was,' said Adam. 'And I have read, or at least dipped into, one of Daniel Goleman's books, *Working with Emotional Intelligence*. I'm amazed that you remember all this stuff. I'm sure I can't keep it in my head. If I have to know all this I'll never get there. In any case, the question is always going to be, "What do I do with the information?" So what's the difference between this EQ and E-Fitness?'

'E-Fitness answers that question, "What do I do with the information?" It's why I liked it so much when I discovered it that I decided to become an E-Fitness coach.' Keith picked up his coffee cup, noticed it was empty and turned for the waitress who happened to be coming over with a pot in her hand. 'Good place, this,' he remarked. 'Emotional Intelligence is essentially a set of questions designed to establish the competencies of an individual based on the criteria established over the years by psychologists trying to understand and explain what in our brains other than our cognitive intelligence causes us to act in certain ways. That's the Emotional Intelligence Quotient, or EQ. Emotional Fitness or E-Fitness is a set of tools that help us to handle our lives in a more positive and healthier way. There are actually nine tools, but we will explore the five that relate more specifically to work, and to the skills that a coach can bring to the table.'

The five tools of E-Fitness coaching

'This is the part where I tell you what I have to offer,' said Keith. 'After that we will return to my original question to you: "What do you want to achieve from this?" That will be our contract with each other.' Keith produced a folder, handed it to Adam and pointed to the front sheet. Adam studied it as Keith took him through the headings.

'You'll see that the first tool relates to what I described last week as the most valuable of the leadership skills. We call it Power Listening. I will tell you about the two things that get in the way of really effective listening and the five things that you can do to become a great listener. You know, if you only do that piece, you will see how things change and how you can become the leader you want to be.

'The second tool that I will teach you, and coach you in, is Learning from Experience. We have a phrase, "learning is earning," that will make sense once you tap into the experience that people have at Baines Electronics. Remember, I won't just be talking about this stuff; you will be practising it and I will coach you through your own experience and learning.'

An image of his conversation with Evelyn shot into Adam's head. He said nothing, leaned over the paper he was holding.

'The third tool,' continued Keith, 'is one that could have special significance for you if you take this promotion. We call it the Group Dialogue. When we combine Power Listening, Learning from Experience and the Group Dialogue, we have E-Fitness Action Learning. It is a way of tapping into the treasure that exists in each member of a team; how we can transform the energy of the individual members of a team into something that works for the whole organization. I know that sounds like very flowery language for what are basically very mundane events. Meetings were the bane of my working existence. I wish I knew then what I know now. I'm just thrilled to have this opportunity to work with you and to see how you might make a real difference.'

'Are you sure you don't want to come back?' asked Adam. 'There's a vacancy for a sales director.'

Keith smiled, ignoring the playful lure. 'The fourth tool we will use is also about energy, this time very much our emotional energy. One of the writers and psychologists I didn't mention is Daniel Pink, who wrote a book called *A Whole New Mind*. Pink is another who points out how much we tend to concentrate on the cognitive portion of our brains at work at the expense of our creative, emotional sides. The fascinating thing is that he shows that it is really an expense on our businesses too. In E-Fitness, the tool that demonstrates and deals with our feeling as distinct from our thinking selves is the Workscale. This is the tool that helps us to explore the inner balance that we have. It's the balance between what satisfies and what frustrates us. We will use it together first. Later I will ask you to use it at work and we will see how you can help people to see that what frustrates them can be turned into some positive, creative action.'

'That sounds just what I need right now,' murmured Adam wistfully.

'Finally,' drove on Keith, 'I will ask you to bring out some of your own creativity and play around with some storytelling. I saw you raise your eyebrows when I mentioned it last time. I just want to tell you that I only expect you to use these tools, any of them, if you find that they work for you. So I offer them for you to try out and accept or reject as you wish. All I know is that they worked for me. I am a different man from the one you knew at work. More accurately, I have learned to be who I really am rather than try to play a part that doesn't feel comfortable.'

'I'm willing to try anything at this point,' Adam said. 'I'd like to get a handle on how this kind of coaching can actually help a business like ours. As I understand it, you are going to be coaching me and I am going to be, at least in part, acting as a coach for others. How is it going to help me if I take on the job as sales director when I hardly feel ready for the job I have just taken on?'

'I can give you an example,' replied Keith. 'The man who introduced me to E-Fitness coaching is a friend of mine. Peter is the human resources director for a large catering company that provides catering services to hospitals, colleges, government offices and big businesses. His company saw its profits diminishing, had staffing problems, experienced increasing wastage and lost thousands of hours through sickness leave because of stress. They wanted to change all that and Peter was given the task of leading the campaign: probably to save the company. After a couple of false starts, one of his business associates recommended a coach to Peter. The coach happened to be an E-Fitness expert. Peter learned all the things I am going to show you and tried them out. He listened to a range of people across the organization, from the managing director to the kitchen staff. He asked people about their specific experiences and what they had learned from them, and how they could apply that learning across the board. He ran meetings in the way I'm going to show you, and he trained managers to run meetings in the same way. He applied the Workscale before and after to a large group of employees. Finally, he ran some storytelling sessions.' Keith paused, took another sip from his now cold second cup of coffee.

Adam filled in the gap expectantly. 'And what happened?'

'Nothing.' Keith looked up and smiled. 'No disaster. No train crash or rocket explosion. No huge apocalypse. But within a year, when the company looked at the results, they found that employee retention rates had increased dramatically, wastage had gone down, the amount of sick leave was reduced significantly and profits spiked at a time of financial constraints. All their targets were exceeded by 20 to 50 per cent. So to answer your question without the irony, what happened was that people, at all levels, felt that they counted for something, that someone was actually listening to them. Although the demands and the pressure of the work were the same, instead of feeling at fault if something went wrong, they discovered that it was okay to discuss and learn from it. They shared ideas from their own experiences and observations and when something got taken up and acknowledged, they were delighted. They wanted to stay, even with the odd hours and relatively low pay, rather than try out another company. They felt part of a place that cared about them, not apart from a place that cared only about profits. The real irony is that profits went up.

'One other interesting example I can mention is that of British Rail. After that accident and the Hidden Report recommendations, they put into place a rigorous system of management and leadership training. Emotional Fitness was in its early days, but the training included much of what we are talking about here. In fact, it was the Power Listening segment that provided the most positive feedback and had the longest-lasting effect, according to many of the managers. I can give you other examples, but in the end you have to decide if you want to try it for yourself.'

The contract

Adam expelled a large breath, as though he had been holding it in for a long time. 'Well, I think my head is spinning. I want to have a go at this. You said you wanted to ask me that question about what I wanted from this and I think I have an answer for you now. First, I want to be clear about whether I will take this new promotion or not. Evelyn gave me two weeks to come back with my answer. Then I want to learn how to listen. In fact, I want to learn all the E-Fitness tools you have talked about and apply them whether I take this job or not.'

'That's very good, Adam,' said Keith. 'That's three things. You want to make a decision; you want to learn the E-Fitness tools, including Power Listening; and you want to apply the tools in your work. Is there anything that you want to achieve for yourself?'

Adam put his head up, stretching back his neck so that he practically looked at the ceiling. 'I want,' he started slowly, then looked at Keith, 'I want to be the kind of person, the kind of leader that I admire. I want to be worthy. I suppose it comes down to respect. I really want to respect myself and know that I am worthy of respect. There: that's it.'

'You want to respect yourself and know that you are worthy of respect,' repeated Keith. 'I'd like you to write down all that you've said here, starting with the three things you said just before and now your last statement. This will be our contract. My part is to offer you the E-Fitness tools; your part is to achieve your goals through the coaching that we do together. We will know you have achieved your goals when you are able to say that you have.'

They both glanced at their watches. Adam couldn't believe how fast the time had gone. It was time for him to leave.

'Next week,' said Keith as they began to move from the table, 'I'd like you to bring that contract back with your own statements written down in it. You will also find a questionnaire about how you see the level of E-Fitness of the company. Bring that back too and we can see what you might want to change and how you can help to bring about that change.'

An exercise

Take a look at the personal learning contract that Adam is completing. To get the best benefit from E-Fitness at work you can follow along with him and complete the contract for yourself. You will also find the Organizational Culture E-Fitness questionnaire. Feel free to complete that too.

E-Fitness personal learning contract

Name..

Date..

Emotional Fitness coaching

Coaching is a dynamic partnership between you and your coach, who is dedicated to inspire you to maximize your personal and professional capacity. Our Emotional Fitness coaches offer you an ongoing opportunity to learn and practise new tools that are uniquely developed to bring greater Emotional Fitness. They are designed to enhance your personal and leadership skills and to enable you to achieve and even go beyond the goals you want in your career, your relationships and your personal success.

Our clients are committed to making positive changes, or are in the process of change and want to handle that change more productively. Others want to discover and unlock whatever it is in their lives that has been holding them back from achieving the success and happiness they want.

All our E-Fitness coaches have taken the required training (minimum 100 hours), have demonstrated their competencies and are licensed by the Emotional Fitness Institute to provide our high-quality brand of coaching.

See our website for a fuller appreciation of our vision and approach and the materials and services available to you.

We abide by the ethical standards of the International Coach Federation.

Section one

We offer the following E-Fitness coaching tools for leaders:

1 Power Listening – helping you to achieve:

   - greater understanding of the effect of listening on the well-being and productivity of employees;

   - high-level skill in listening to others;

   - more clarity in how to achieve your goals as a leader;

   - clearer understanding of your personal attributes and concerns;

   - a plan to integrate what you have learned in order to bring about positive change.

2 Learning from Experience – helping you to:

   - draw out your and others' strengths from personal experience;

   - learn how to change past bad experiences into new successful behaviour;

   - build up a portfolio of positive attributes;

   - gain greater self-confidence and esteem.

3 Group Dialogue – teaching you how to:

   - bring out the best talent in your team;

   - facilitate meetings that are productive and creative;

   - develop a culture of listening, learning and positive action.

4 Workscale – enabling you to:

   - understand your level of inner balance;

   - recognize how you can use your satisfactions more effectively;

   - transform your frustrations into positive, creative action;

   - provide a developmental tool to use as a coach.

5 Storytelling – providing you with:

   - a dynamic, fun way to draw out valuable personal insights;

   - a tool to encourage personal accountability;

   - a communication process to generate new understanding between people.

Section two – for you to complete
This is what I commit to achieving for myself through my E-Fitness coaching:

1   My own personal development:

2   My own professional development:

Organizational Culture E-Fitness questionnaire

Rate each question on how satisfied you are. Scores are:

5 if you are extremely satisfied;

4 if you have a high level of satisfaction;

3 if you are reasonably satisfied;

2 if you are dissatisfied;

1 if you are very dissatisfied with the situation.

Section one: communication

1 How good are people at talking to one another in the organization? ....

2 How good are people at listening to each other? ....

3 How good are people at passing on information? ....

4 How much openness exists? ....

5 How well do people give and receive direct feedback? ....

6 How well do meetings work? ....

7 How good is the communication across and between hierarchies? ....

8 How good is the communication between customers and the organization? ....

9 How well do people share ideas? ....

10 How well is conflict dealt with? ....

Section two: finance

11 How well are salary/wage differentials worked out?   ....

12 How close to functions are levels of budgetary responsibility?   ....

13 Is there good accountability for spending and earning?   ....

14 Is financial information shared?   ....

15 Are there profit-sharing schemes?   ....

16 Are there other positive financial incentives?   ....

Section three: decision taking

17 Are decisions taken at appropriate levels?   ....

18 Is there a good consultation process?   ....

19 How well are decisions communicated?   ....

20 Are decisions implemented effectively?   ....

Section four: staff development

21 Are there positive equal opportunities policy and practice?   ....

22 Is there a career development process for staff?   ....

23 Is there a good recruitment and selection process?   ....

24 What is the orientation process like?   ....

25 Do people learn in the organization?   ....

26 Are there good opportunities for training and education?   ....

27   Is coaching a normal part of managers' duties?   ....

28   Is there a positive appraisal system in operation?   ....

29   Is there a satisfactory grievance procedure for staff?   ....

30   How are disciplinary issues dealt with?   ....

31   Is there a staff care programme?   ....

32   Is there a counselling, coaching or mentoring programme?   ....

33   Is there a good exit interview process?   ....

Section five: the work environment

34   Are the work surroundings and conditions safe, pleasant and
     healthy?   ....

35   Is there adequate consultation about the work environment?   ....

36   Is action carried out promptly to improve conditions when
     needed?   ....

37   Do people take on responsibility for their own work
     environment?   ....

38   Are there good facilities for people for rest, health and
     recreation?   ....

Section six: community

39   Is there good contact with the surrounding community?   ....

40   Is there an involvement with the local community?   ....

Total score   ....

What is your satisfaction rating of the organization's culture? The total scores give you a rough guide as to how you think it is doing.

If you gave 40–80, why are you still there? Not much is likely to change.

A score of 81–100 shows that some radical rethinking is needed, but there may be a chance.

101–120 indicates plenty of room for improvement.

121–160 shows an organization with a very positive culture.

If you have 161–200, you work in the perfect organization; or you're kidding!

Make a summary of what you would like to improve.

Power Listening

02

If you want to be
a great
communicator,
listen up

Normal conversation is not communication

After Adam finished filling in his responses to the questionnaire that Keith had given him, he sat back in his seat, feeling the vibration of the train as it sped along the tracks. Was he really cut out for management? If you had to think about all that stuff, when was there time for work? He smiled at his own thought patterns, embarrassed that he had asked himself those questions. What had Keith said? 'If you just get that listening piece right, you will see how things change and you will be a good leader.' Answering the questionnaire had been an eye-opener. He didn't think Baines was a bad company; in fact, he always thought it was run well. But the first section on communication showed him how much room there was for improvement. He thought back to his conversation with Evelyn the day before.

'Adam,' she had begun, 'I know you are thinking about taking on my role as sales director and I gave you a couple of weeks to think about it. I thought it would be a good idea to discuss what the job entails and for me to get your ideas on how you would tackle it.'

'I'd appreciate that,' said Adam. 'It seems such a big jump after just getting used to the idea of being regional sales manager.'

'Yes, well; it's the same for me, really. I've only been in this position for six months and now I'm to take on the company. We are all going to have to step up. As I see it, the sales director's job is about motivation, much like the regional sales manager's is. The only difference is that you need to have a grasp of the bigger picture. The other thing is that you must be ready to talk with high-level customers, especially from overseas as we start to expand. And of course you have to develop a solid strategy to achieve the sales targets that we set for the company, which means that you and I will have to work together closely.'

Adam started to feel out of his depth. He had to say something. 'Um, does it mean that I would have to travel and be out of the country much?'

Evelyn gave him a withering look. 'If that's what's needed, of course. Look Adam, this is a big job, and it's going to grow. I think you're up to it, but you'll have to make some sacrifices to get anywhere and to get the company where it needs to be. It also means you are going to have to get tough with some of our sales team. I've been looking at the figures and we seem to be carrying a few people who aren't pulling their weight. Quite apart from that, we are going to have to hire a few more if we are going to expand the way we intend. The trouble is, we have to have quick results because there will be a cash flow problem if the sales team doesn't come up with the results.'

'I've been thinking about that,' said Adam.

'Good. You might also want to come up with some ideas for a person who will replace you; and someone who is going to concentrate on the overseas side. I think we need someone to focus on that specifically. How about putting a few ideas together and letting me have them in a day or two?'

Evelyn turned to her computer. The meeting appeared to be over. Adam left her office.

Mulling this over, Adam reflected that he had given low scores in the communication section based on that conversation, and that it had been similar to most he had experienced over his time at Baines. He had never given it much thought before. Now, he understood what Keith had been saying to him. He had not felt listened to, nor had he been able to say what he wanted. He felt inept, whereas going into the meeting he had ideas that he wanted to share and questions that he thought were valuable to ask. Was it he who was emotionally unfit or Evelyn? Probably both of them; but it only mattered that he was. And then he thought a little further; and the thought was the most uncomfortable one he'd had so far. He thought that he wasn't very different from Evelyn in the way that he spoke to and listened to others. The train arrived, mercifully, at its destination.

A Power Listening conversation

'Let's see,' said Keith in response to Adam's first question that morning. 'What motivates you?'

'Hmm. Interesting that you put it back to me. I think there are two general ways I get motivated. One is when someone tells me to get something done and if I don't there will be consequences. That could be something as mundane as paying the electricity bill. If I don't do it, they'll cut me off. Or if I fail to pick up the cleaning on Friday when I promised to, my wife would be really upset with me. Then there's the kind of motivation I get when I really want to do something, especially if it's a challenge. So the first is based on punishment, or the threat of it, and the second is more to do with inspiration.'

'Wonderful summary of motivation theory,' smiled Keith. 'The carrot or the stick theory, reward or punishment: old as the hills and as true as ever. Tell me which works best for you.'

'In a way they both work, but I know which I enjoy the most.'

'And now tell me,' said Keith, leaning forward a little, 'which of the two do you tend to receive and give out at work?'

Adam coloured slightly. 'Well, based on my conversation with Evelyn, which was about as typical as it gets, I'd say that it is usually the stick, even if it's disguised. And I'd also have to admit I probably do the same. Come to think of it, the only person at Baines who always seems inspired is Marcus Baines.'

Keith leant forward a little more over the coffee table until his tie brushed his coffee cup. 'How would I know what inspires you?'

'You'd have to ask me. And you'd have to listen. And I'd have to know.'

'Just so,' murmured Keith, and leaned back in his chair. 'I am going to ask you. I will listen. And as I listen, you will know, if you don't already, what inspires you. But since these sessions are also about teaching you the basics of E-Fitness coaching, I will describe Power

Listening to you as well, since it is the foundation of everything else that we do.'

'I'm ready for that,' said Adam. 'I've been intrigued since you mentioned it. And if I can really find out what inspires me it will be a bonus. Problem with that is, it might not fit into the work I'm doing and the job that I have been offered. Let's go for it anyway.'

'As you say, "Let's go for it." First of all, you have already seen that what motivates you in a positive, healthy way – or, as you described it, in an inspirational way, as opposed to when you feel you will be punished if you don't do something – begins when you are able to express what you want. For that, somebody has to listen.'

Keith paused. It gave Adam the chance to absorb this seemingly insignificant statement. As he did so, its significance seemed to grow. He thought of his wife. Pauline was the only one in his life who listened. Even with her, he didn't take home most of the worries he had about work. He couldn't think of a time when he had really talked to her, or anyone, about himself in any meaningful sense. They talked about doing things, and the children and work in a general sense. But he never talked about what he really wanted. What did he want?

Keith resumed. 'E-Fitness coaching, and Power Listening in particular, is based on the belief that we all have our own wisdom about ourselves and our possibilities within us, and that much of the time we don't know it. We don't know it because it's hard to hear ourselves, so we need someone to listen it out of us. And because most people don't know how to listen, we need a coach to start us off.'

'Why don't people know how to listen?' asked Adam.

'Glad you asked that. Two reasons. The first is that they get in the way. The second is nobody taught them how.'

'What do you mean, "they get in the way"?'

'Well, think what might get in the way of you really listening to someone else. Start with someone you know.'

'There's my wife, Pauline. She does tell me that I don't listen to her, although I really try.'

'Very well. I'm not judging you here; simply wanting you to understand what goes on, and there's no better way than understanding what goes on for you. Give me an example of when you found yourself not listening to her as well as you'd have liked.'

'Yesterday evening when I came home, she was talking to me about her day with the kids. Mark is four and spends the morning at kindergarten and Anna is two. They can be quite a handful. Anyway, I was probably distracted, but I noticed that I didn't respond to her much and she got quite upset with me. But I was listening to her.'

'You were distracted and didn't respond to her much. What was going on for you?'

'You know, I'm feeling under a lot of pressure at work and I suppose it was at the back of my mind.' Adam stopped.

Keith said nothing. A few seconds ticked by. Adam felt a trickle of perspiration in his armpits. He started to speak again, his voice a little lower.

'To tell you the truth, I was feeling pissed off with Pauline. Frankly, I felt that her day with our children was nothing compared with what I'm going through right now. It's not as though she doesn't know. She says she'd like to go back to work. Sometimes I'd just like to stay at home with the kids. Of course, we can't afford for me not to have this job; and the opportunity I've been offered will make a big difference financially to us. I just don't think Pauline acknowledges that.'

'You've said some important things here, Adam; things that so easily get in the way of your being able to listen to Pauline. Remember, this is just an example – although I understand it's a very real one – of how hard it is to listen. Pauline starts to tell you something about her day, clearly wanting you to listen to her. You feel angry and resentful because she is apparently not listening to what you are not saying. Is that right?'

'Yes, that's about it.' Adam shifted uncomfortably in his chair.

'In other words, you were getting in the way. Let's take another example, this time the one you told me about earlier, when Evelyn and you were having a conversation. This time, as I recall, it seems that you are the one who didn't feel listened to. Tell me what you think may have been going on for Evelyn. Of course, this can only be your own guess, but it may give you some indication of how she was getting in the way of being able to listen to you.'

'One of the first things she said was that she wanted to hear my ideas. Then as soon as I started by saying it was a big jump for me, she said it was the same for her. Basically she was telling me to lump it, although she never said anything like that.'

'When she said it was the same for her, what was she doing? How do you think she was getting in her own way of being able to listen to you?'

Adam thought for a moment. 'She picked up what I said and basic-ally took it away from me. She might have intended to show she understood because she was in the same situation, but what happened was that she discounted how it affected me. After all, our situations are very different. We're very different.' Adam slowed down, his brow furrowed; he pursed his lips. 'I just realized that I did the same to Pauline, although in this case I never said anything. Pauline was telling me she'd had a bad day, and I was thinking "My day was worse." So I didn't listen to her.'

'You got in the way, just as Evelyn got in the way instead of being able to listen to you. Essentially, this is what happens in almost every human interaction. It doesn't matter whether it's personal or profes-sional, whether the topic is the weather or world peace, we get in the way of being able to pay full attention to one another. It's not inten-tional; it's simply a lack of mindfulness. Instead of listening to another, we hear the voices in our own head. The voices are all ours, of course, but they are the ones we have adopted. They are the voices of our critics, past and present, of our teachers, of others whom we know or don't know, people we admire or despise. They may appear to be tell-ing us what we are supposed to be saying or how we should behave. As well as those voices, and perhaps even stronger, are our own fears and hopes and desires that can overtake our ability to listen to one another. What you say can trigger a fear in me, so I respond from that fear. For example, your comment to Evelyn about your fear of taking that jump into such a quick promotion may have triggered her own feelings. Of course, I'm only surmising that and I don't want to delve into someone else's psychology, nor do we need to. It's just an illus-tration of how we get in the way.'

Adam nodded, consciously trying to listen without having his own thoughts block off what Keith was telling him.

His coach continued. 'The irony is that each of us has a strong desire to be truly listened to, to be heard, to be understood, to be accepted and to be encouraged by others. I'm going to take you through that again in detail later. Before that, I want you to tell me what you understand now by "getting in the way" of listening.'

Adam nodded again, then shook his head briskly, suddenly aware that he was expected to respond.

'This really makes sense,' he began. 'You mean that most of the time someone looks as though they are listening to another person, they are really listening to their own problems.' He noticed Keith's glance and hastily added, 'Or not problems necessarily; maybe their ideas or thoughts on the subject. Certainly their own experience gets in the way. I could also see that someone in a higher position might want to have a say if only to maintain their status; maybe that's what Evelyn was doing. And in my case with Pauline, I was feeling indignant that she saw her day as more difficult than mine, so I couldn't listen to her, or at least I didn't want to acknowledge her problems. I can think of another way that I don't listen to Pauline.'

'What's that?' asked Keith.

'When she has some question or problem or other, and I respond to her, she can get angry and then tells me that I'm not listening. I've always had difficulty with that, because I think I'm listening really well and I'm just coming up with some answers or advice that seem obvious to me. Now I can see that I'm just getting in the way of her solving her own problems; or "working it through" as she says.'

'You're getting the hang of this, Adam. What all this adds up to, all those "voices in the head" egging us on and the fears or desires that stop us hearing one another, is our emotional self getting in the way. We can listen intellectually and respond intelligently, just as Evelyn did to you and you did to Pauline. But the emotional side prevented either of you from listening fully and cleanly. Our emotional self is the most primitive part of our being and kicks in without us usually being conscious of it. It makes us fearful or angry, or depressed or ecstatic. Often we don't like the emotions, and don't want to show or even admit to them. Then what happens is they can have an effect on us mentally or physically. So if you feel anxious, you may break out into a sweat or have a headache. When you even think about doing something that scares you, like standing up and addressing a crowd of 2,000 people, your stomach might turn inside out. Take a look at Gabor Maté's book, *When the Body Says No, understanding the stress – disease connection* to understand how much our emotions affect our health and our behaviour.

'Now I want you to imagine what it would be like in either of those scenarios you described earlier if Evelyn listened to you and you listened to your wife without either of you getting in the way. What would happen?'

'You mean if the emotions didn't get in the way?'

Keith nodded.

'Well, if Evelyn had listened to me it would have given me a chance to give her some of my ideas and ask some questions. I would probably have blurted out that I was scared to death of taking this job and needed a lot of hand-holding; so I suppose that wouldn't have looked very good.'

'What would make it not look very good?'

'You don't want to tell your boss that you're not cut out for a promotion, do you? I mean, what is she going to think?'

Keith said nothing. Adam struggled with the silence, knowing that he had to answer his own questions.

Taking a deep breath, he ploughed on. 'I suppose if I didn't let my emotional self get in the way I would be able to say what was on my mind; and if Evelyn didn't let herself get in the way, she would be able to listen without putting any judgements up. Or does it mean that if I were emotionally fit I wouldn't have any fears about this job anyway?' As soon as the words were out of his mouth, he knew with certainty that Keith was not going to answer the question. 'Okay,' submitted Adam, 'I get it. It doesn't mean I wouldn't have any emotions, like feeling fearful. It means that I could handle them better and talk about them; within reason anyway.'

A sense of smugness spread through Adam as he thought about what he had just uttered. He really was getting it. Except for one thing.

'The big question for me is: how do you get out of the way?' He gazed at Keith, willing him to answer this one.

Keith obliged, ducking his head to one side as though waiting for a word of wisdom to come from above. 'That is the big question. The best way I can answer it is to say that we can get ourselves out of the way when we have understood well enough what does get in the way and have the tools to deal with it. We must become more aware, more conscious, or as I prefer to call it, more mindful of what our own needs and hopes and fears are to the extent that we can set them aside for the time being when we are listening to another. In order to do that, we have to be able to express ourselves to someone else who will listen to us. That's another one of those ironies. The really good news for you is that this is exactly what a good coach can do, especially an E-Fitness coach. This takes us exactly to the point where I shall listen to you. There was a question about what inspires you, I believe.'

'Yes, you're right,' said Adam. 'It's interesting that I wasn't really aware of that question until I began to think about it after our conversations and doing that contract for myself. But then it kept coming up. What do I want? What motivates me? And finally, what gives me inspiration?'

'That is your question for yourself. My job now is to listen to you, without getting in the way so that you may answer your question. I won't be giving you any advice and I won't be critical or offer any judgement. What I will do at times is to ask you questions for greater clarification and help you make sense of your own thoughts. And at any time, I am open to you letting me know if something I do or say doesn't work for you. Now, tell me a bit more about what your question means to you.'

Adam began slowly. 'I think it's a question I've always had. What do I really want? It seems now that the question is more about what inspires me. I'm not the kind of person who feels much inspiration, I suppose. But I do notice and envy others who show it. I mentioned Marcus Baines. I know he owns the company, but he's someone who seems to be interested in everything and everyone and who is always looking at new possibilities. There's a rumour that he is always in the building before seven every morning and wanders around looking for new ideas. I'd like to feel as inspired as him.'

'Can you describe to me what that feeling of inspiration is like?'

'I imagine it's a feeling of loving something so much that you want to be up and about before anyone else just to savour it.'

'Ever felt like that?'

Adam hesitated. He smiled. 'My kids. When those two little things rush into our room in the morning this amazing feeling comes over me. I can hardly imagine that I've brought these two children into the world and that I'm responsible, with my wife of course, for bringing them up in it. It's just a fleeting feeling and I don't give myself much time to think about it; in fact, I usually get up before they do these days. But now I think about it, I'm inspired that I am the father of these two lovely kids.'

'What is it exactly that brings you this inspiration?'

Adam pictured them, Mark and Anna, jumping up and down in their excitement of being alive. That brought him a lot of pleasure, but it wasn't that. 'I know what it is,' he said. 'It's that I get to teach them about life. I want to keep them safe and at the same time to show them the possibilities. It's my job to give them the best possible start in life. Now that inspires me.'

'You talked about possibilities earlier.'

'Did I?'

'Yes, when you were talking about Marcus Baines. You said that he was always looking for possibilities. Now you say that you are inspired because it's your job to teach your children about life, to keep them safe and show them possibilities.'

Adam had only heard the expression 'a light went on in his brain' before. He had never experienced it until this moment. 'The factory is Marcus Baines's child,' he exclaimed. 'We are his children. He feels responsible for keeping us safe; or in a job anyway, and showing us what's possible. And that gives him inspiration.'

'That's Marcus Baines. What do you get from it for yourself?'

The words flowed from Adam as though they had been pent up and suddenly the dam had burst. 'Until I had children I never had, or felt, the responsibility for teaching or showing anyone anything of real worth. My kids are giving me the chance to do that; and of course they trust me totally. That's one thing I love: being trusted. I am trustworthy, but it hardly ever feels as though I am trusted or respected. That's another story. I know it's held me back. Here it is, Keith. I am inspired when I can show what's possible to others when I know that they trust and respect me. Ouch.'

'What was the "ouch" for?'

'Because it brings up some fear. What if I am not trusted?'

'That is certainly a question for us to explore, and we will. For now I want to make sure I have understood what you have said. What gives you inspiration is when you show others what is possible. You have learned that from your children. You also believe that in order to show possibilities to others, they have to trust and respect you and you are uncertain whether that can be so. Is that right?'

'Yes, that's just it.' Adam's voice rose up an octave. 'I want to add one thing, though. It's not enough for me to show what's possible; I want to see the results. I have to see that what I showed had some impact and that it changed something for the better. For example, the other day I heard Mark tell his little sister that their mummy needed a little peace and quiet. I knew where that came from and I knew that he noticed that Pauline was tired. That's pretty good for a four-year-old, and I'm proud that I had been able to show him that.'

'With that important addition, Adam, how do propose to use this information about yourself and what inspires you?'

'I'm feeling excited and scared at the same time as I say this. I'm going to take that promotion, and my job will be to show others what's possible and to gain their trust. Funny thing is, the excitement is my inspiration and my fear is about whether I can trust myself enough to pull it off.'

Keith grinned at Adam. 'On that note, I see that the time has flown by and it's time for you to go. As always, I'd like you to note down the essence of what you have said here, along with any questions you have for next time. Anything you want to say before we finish?'

'This is fantastic. You really did keep out of the way and I answered my own questions. I still don't know how you did that. What I know now is that that's what I want to do too.'

'We'll go through that next time. You may have some more to tell me then. Practise listening to your wife too.'

Preparing to change

Matthew finished screwing the new nameplate onto Evelyn's door and stood back, not so much to admire his handiwork, but rather to study the new inscription. The name 'Evelyn Young' above the title 'Sales Director' was now 'Evelyn Baines-Young' without any title. He grimaced, shook his head slowly and tucked the screwdriver back into his tool belt. Nobody told him anything. Didn't stop him knowing. He whistled his way to the next job on today's maintenance list.

Evelyn sat in one of the two easy chairs in Marcus Baines's office. The other was occupied by the owner.

'What's the news, my dear?' Marcus had learned to be careful about his language when he addressed other female members of staff, but Evelyn was his niece and was truly dear to him. He knew the feeling was reciprocated. Hadn't he practically been a father for her after Trevor died so suddenly when she was still a baby?

'Good, I think,' said Evelyn. She wanted to add 'Marcus' but was still finding it hard to drop the 'Uncle' as he had insisted. 'We're in business now,' he'd said, with one of his impish grins, 'and nobody else calls me Uncle Marcus here.'

'Adam dropped in to see me this morning,' she continued. 'He said he had decided to take the position as sales director when I step into your role in six months.'

'Excellent, excellent,' gushed Marcus. 'And why do you express some doubt about that?'

'I've only just brought him on as regional sales manager and I thought that was a bit of a risk. I'm not sure he's ready for this big step.'

'Nonsense. He'll be fine. And you have six months to get him acclimatized. After all, the job itself is only six months' old, so you've been making it up. And I handled it all before that. Adam's a good lad: quick learner. Hasn't he had the best sales figures for two years running?' Marcus looked at his watch.

'True, but this is a leadership position at a very crucial time. When you retire it will leave a big gap, and we have to put sound management and sales teams in place in order to grow the business. My concern about Adam is that the other sales managers aren't going to respect him. When I got rid of Patrick and replaced him with Adam there were rumblings. I can imagine what they'll say when they hear I'm making him their boss. They didn't like it when I came in.'

'Oh, they'll be all right. Anyway, you already offered him the post and he's accepted. Just have to get on with it now. I suppose you told him to keep it quiet; don't want people to know I'm going just yet.'

'Of course. Adam had to know the situation and that it's confidential until we make an official announcement.'

'Very good.' Marcus glanced at his watch again. 'Anything else?'

Evelyn didn't notice the new nameplate as she returned to her office, closing the door behind her. She sat behind her desk, swivelling the chair until she looked out of her window at the cars below. Her head was throbbing.

* * * * * *

Pauline watched her husband as he crawled around the floor with his daughter on his back and his son sitting on his ankles, both of them laughing while Adam bellowed like an elephant.

'You're an amazing dad,' she told him later.

'I love being a dad,' he replied. 'And I want to be a better husband.'

'You're not so bad,' she said, and kissed him on the ear.

'But I can be better. I'm going to try to listen to you better.'

She looked at him closely, studying his face. 'It's those conversations you've been having with Keith, isn't it? Well, if it benefits me I can't say I mind. But seriously, Adam, now that you've decided to take on that job I do understand the extra work and pressure it's going to take. I should be listening to you.'

'All I can say is, you're an amazing wife,' said Adam.

The five stages of Power Listening – the need to grow

Springtime was fully in the air. Daffodils and tulips abounded in the park. Adam and Keith had decided to meet on their original bench this morning. This time Adam's spirit rose as he saw the tall man approaching.

'Lots to tell you,' began Adam. 'I told Evelyn that I'd take the job. My heart was in my mouth and I could hardly believe I was saying it. I realized two things. One is that when an opportunity like that comes up I'd be crazy not to take it, whatever happens. The other is that I could really get to be inspired if I see the job as motivating others and showing them the possibilities. So,' exclaimed Adam with a note of triumph in his voice, 'I have carried out the first item on my contract.'

'Congratulations, Adam,' said Keith, not making it clear exactly which of Adam's statements he was being congratulated for.

Adam went on as though he were on a runaway cycle. 'Pauline and I had a great conversation about it. She really supports me. And I told her that I wanted to listen to her better. A funny thing happened after that: she said she should be listening to me and I started talking about a lot of the stuff you and I had discussed; about inspiration and things like that. Anyway, I didn't do what I really hoped, which was to listen to her. She did that for me, though, and I talked more to her than I have for a long time. I'm not sure what happened there. I'll try again next time. I know that I can get out of the way when I think about it.'

The cycle seemed to slow down and come to a halt. Adam crossed his legs.

'Yes, I believe you can,' mused Keith almost to himself. 'Now it's time to move on. You said that what happened with Pauline was a funny thing, and you described how you came to the decision to take on that job. I'm going to tell you about the five stages of Power Listening and I believe you will recognize what has been happening. You might also recall our last session when you spoke and I listened to you talk about inspiration. I was using Power Listening then. Please interject at any time to ask questions or to let me know when you make a connection with what you have experienced.'

A butterfly wafted by and they both watched it for a moment. Adam wondered about the truth of the butterfly effect in chaos theory: a butterfly flaps its wings and eventually causes a hurricane on the other side of the earth. He settled himself to listen to Keith.

'I said the other day that there are two things that get in the way of great listening. One is us getting in the way, and we explored that. The other is that there is little understanding about the actual process of listening and what it entails. There are actually five stages in Power Listening and that's what I want to teach you. As you have already gathered, I am both a coach and a teacher for you for the purposes of having you understand and use E-Fitness coaching in your work.

'As an E-Fitness coach, my role is to listen to and draw out your own wisdom. It is an empowering process, meaning that the expertise of the coach is in the process, whereas the client is the expert in his or her own life. At the same time, in E-Fitness coaching, the actual tools are offered to the client to use. For example, I not only listen to you, I also show you how to listen to yourself. You asked last time how one gets out of the way when listening to others. Part of the answer is that you have learned to listen to yourself. That is the real key to understanding what inspires you, to appreciating your strengths and understanding your weaknesses and to being able to empower yourself to take the action that you desire.

'Power Listening was developed through observing some of the great listeners of the 20th century and making sense of what they were actually doing. It was also a result of what so many people expressed that was missing for them in most relationships in their personal or working lives. Here is what we need as human beings in order to become the best we can be; or in being able to see and reach the possibilities, as you might like to put it.'

Keith paused. Adam seemed oblivious to the pair of joggers who went past them, or the bee that buzzed around their heads, or the constant hissing of spray from the water fountain.

'We need,' continued Keith, 'to be listened to.'

If Adam was disappointed with that statement, he didn't show it. Instead, he craned his neck forward ready to receive more.

His teacher went on. 'We have a need to express what is important for us, and for that we need someone to listen it out of us. But not only do we need to be listened to; we need to be heard, and heard in a way that lets us know that what we believe to be important, really is, and that it's respected rather than judged as insignificant. We have two needs so far: being listened to and being heard. The third is that we need to be understood. Now, when I talk about needs, I'm not talking about the physical, biological hierarchy of needs that we all know about. I'm talking about the need for our emotional growth: our E-Fitness. Being understood, even by just one person, can be an almost ecstatic experience, it is so rare. The fourth thing that we need is to be and to feel accepted. Here, I am not talking about the social acceptance that most people crave; I mean the acceptance of our thoughts, feelings, beliefs and behaviour in a way that validates us, even when the other person doesn't subscribe to the same thoughts or beliefs. Acceptance doesn't mean agreement. It does mean respect, which is something you have referred to a few times. Finally, while we need to be listened to, heard, understood and accepted, we also need to have encouragement, or a positive response. That response is going on all the time. The difference here is that the response in Power Listening is the one that takes us forward: to achieve those possibilities you talked about. Those are the five things we need for us to attain E-Fitness. The aim for the E-Fitness coach is for you to be able to listen, hear, understand and accept yourself and to respond accordingly.

'Power Listening is powerful. That means that it's dynamic and active. So we have to go beyond what is needed and provide some actions that match the needs.'

The five stages of Power Listening – the action steps

1. To listen, set the contract

Adam uncrossed his legs and took his hand away from his chin. It was the first movement he had made for some time and now his body surged animatedly.

'Sounds like this is the bit I've been waiting for. I just want to see if I've got this part right so far, though. You seem to be saying that listening is more than just listening. It starts with that, but you also have to hear what's being said and understand it. And you have to show that you accept what the person is saying and somehow make a response. I'm a bit hazy about how this goes. But you're going to tell me how to do it, right?'

'I am,' Keith asserted. 'I am also going to refer back to our conversation about inspiration last time so that you can see what I was doing – apart, of course, from getting out of your way. The first thing that the E-Fitness coach does in Power Listening is to set up a contract. Remember when you and I first did that? What happened?'

Adam screwed up his eyes. 'Let me see. You told me it was confidential. And you asked me what I wanted to talk about, and what I wanted to get from the conversation. You also told me that being my boss in a past life wouldn't be a problem or something like that.'

'Yes, good. And what effect did that have on you?'

'Well, I hadn't known what to expect. It was a relief to have your assurances and I was a bit surprised to have you ask what I wanted to get out of it. I was a little stumped at first, but it made me think.'

'Anything else that you felt or experienced from that very first part, before you even started to talk?'

'As I said, I felt relieved and surprised at the same time. It felt safe too, even if it was a challenge to have to think about myself.'

'What felt safe?'

'It felt safe that I could talk to you and you would listen. Ah, I'm getting something now. I don't remember having this feeling before, but I felt as though I could say anything. Actually it felt liberating. I started thinking about what I really wanted. I remember asking you a lot of questions. I think I was checking you out, you know, to see if you really would listen to me. I had this inkling that I wanted to say that I didn't have a clear idea of what I want, what inspires me, but I wasn't ready to say that. It helped that we had a break before I got into that and finished my side of the contract. That piece about inspiration was something I hadn't ever looked at, but it seemed absolutely right when I talked about it and discovered it in my children.'

Keith spread his hands out, palms upwards. 'There you have it, Adam. The contract begins the process of listening. It starts the ball rolling for you to know that you will be listened to. Even more important, or rather as a natural part of that, you start to listen to yourself clearly. Now tell me,' continued Keith, 'when you told me about that conversation you had with Evelyn when you said she didn't listen to you, where was the contract?'

'There wasn't one.'

'And when you talked to Pauline when you said something funny happened?'

'I was supposed to listen to her, and she said she should listen to me, and then she asked me how I was feeling about work and the big decision. So I didn't have a contract to listen to her; she had one with me. And she doesn't even know about this stuff!'

'Isn't that something? Remember that Power Listening isn't based on psychological or theoretical concepts; it is based on observation of what really good listeners do naturally. Sounds like your wife is a natural. Let's go back to that conversation with Evelyn. What kind of contract could you have had?'

'I have no idea. I mean, she's the boss. Wouldn't she have to establish the rules?'

Keith cocked his head to one side, said nothing.

'Oh, very well,' laughed Adam. 'I'm getting the hang of this. I have to answer my own questions. I suppose if I have something to say to her, or ask her, then I could just say that. You mean that it doesn't have to be the person listening who has to set up the contract; it can be the person who wants to be listened to? Silly me, you didn't say anything. I'm right, aren't I?'

It was Keith's turn to laugh. 'You are going to make a great E-Fitness coach, Adam. The beauty is that if you use these methods as the new sales director, nobody will see you as a coach; they will just feel inspired by you; and you will have their trust and respect. Anyway, to summarize this, in order to listen or be listened to, you have to set a contract.'

'When you say "set a contract", what are the kinds of things that you'd do?' queried Adam. 'You know the sort of people who work at Baines. They're all great – well, mostly – but nobody's got time for stuff that isn't pretty straightforward and to the point. I mean, we're in the business of electronics, not art therapy or something equally esoteric.'

'Which is why setting a contract can be so valuable, Adam. Let's go back to that conversation you had with Evelyn. We can assume that she won't change her style at this point; so it's up to you. What are some of the things that you would like to see in any contract you set up for that meeting with her?'

'You always make me work it out, Keith.'

'That's why it's called coaching,' said Keith. 'Are you going to work it out?'

'I'll have a go. Something very basic. I'd like to have known how much time we had, or maybe to negotiate the time. Then I wouldn't have been surprised when the discussion just finished.' Adam looked at Keith.

'Absolutely. Sometimes it's as basic as things like that. The fact is that the basics seldom happen, so people don't know where they are. It also means that the person leading the conversation holds all the power. Not much listening takes place in those circumstances; just posturing. What else?'

'I think I could have asked for what I wanted. I wanted to talk about my ideas and my doubts. I suppose I could have said that to Evelyn. It's not as though she's an unreasonable person, and she probably has her own doubts too. More than anything, I think I wanted to be clear about what she expected of me and what kind of support I can get from her.'

Keith smiled. 'There you have the beginnings of a contract that lays out in a much clearer fashion what kind of relationship you could have and what your communication can be like. When you are able to say what you want and ask the other person what she wants from the conversation, and then you negotiate the time you both need, you are setting up a contract. What's not straightforward and to the point there?'

Adam inclined his head to the rhetorical question. 'So, before we even talk about anything, we discuss talking about it.'

'In a way, yes.'

'So how and when do we decide what we're going to talk about? And what about the listening bit?'

'The listening bit, as you call it, is part of the contract. It's important when saying what you want, that you would like to be listened to, and that you will listen to the other if that's what they want. As to what you talk about, you are exactly on cue for our second stage in Power Listening.'

2. To hear, focus on the issue

'You'll recall,' continued Keith, 'that listening actually starts with the contract. Do you remember those five things that we need in order to become emotionally fit? To be listened to is the first.'

'To be heard is the second.' Adam had read up on his notes.

'Excellent,' burst out Keith, and they both glowed in a brief moment of some rarely remembered glory. 'Now I want to take us back again to our own conversation. It began when you were asking about what motivates people and I asked you what motivates you. You immediately started to muse about that.'

'Yes,' said Adam, 'it was something I'd been thinking about because I realized that it was going to be a big part of my new job; either of the jobs, actually.'

'You had also decided that you could talk to me about it, because we had established a contract beforehand. You knew I would listen to you. The question was, would I be able and willing to hear what you really wanted to say?'

Adam frowned. 'I certainly hoped so.'

'The real test,' continued Keith 'is whether or not I can help you to focus on what's important for you. For you, notice – not for me. Since you came up with the word "motivation", that's what I asked you about. I wanted to hear what was on your mind and before I even asked you, you told me. Quite often, it takes a little longer to discover what the other person wants to focus on. The point is, you can only really hear what someone else is presenting when they focus on what's important to them and when you do that too.'

'It all happened so seamlessly when you did it. When I talked to Evelyn it was as though I couldn't get my words or even my thoughts together because it moved very quickly from what was on my mind to what was on hers. If she was going to hear me, assuming as you said, she wasn't going to change, I would have to say to her what exactly I wanted to talk about.'

'That's precisely it. It's more difficult when you are the one who wants to be listened to. As the listener, or the E-Fitness coach, you are the one who can provide the framework of Power Listening. This second phase is, like the others, simple and highly effective because of its simplicity. Listen to most conversations. How often do you hear someone ask another to spell out what is the most important thing for them to focus on and talk about?'

There was a pause and Adam recognized that Keith didn't ask a question in order to answer it himself. It was up to Adam to respond.

'Well, seldom, I suppose,' he answered. 'And now I come to think of it, I can't recall it ever happening at work. It's always the person who is speaking who wants to make a point, not to ask others. And that's usually the person who is higher up on the management scale. When I completed that organization culture questionnaire, I knew that communication left something to be desired. I recall giving a fairly high rating for talking, but not much for listening. Now I understand why. My challenge is to see if I can change some of that.'

'And the beauty of this,' added Keith, 'is that you don't have to throw the spectre of change in people's faces, as though they are doing something wrong now. All you need to do is to put this Power Listening into play and see what happens. Now you have the first two phases. Establish a contract, or, to put it another way, make it clear that you will be listening; the second is to help the other person to focus on what is important for them so that you can hear what they have to say.'

'This sounds really easy.'

'It is,' returned Keith. 'The fact is, it's also difficult. What has exercised my mind over the past couple of years since I've been learning this, is how come something so simple can be so hard for people to do? As we discussed the other day, it must be because we get in the way, and we haven't had a framework to use. Now let me go on to the third part of Power Listening. Remember what we need after being listened to and heard?'

Adam struggled to recall, bringing up a picture of his notes. He gave up and allowed himself to imagine what he wanted from Pauline when he was talking to her. His wife did seem to be a natural at this. Of course! 'We need to be understood.' He knew he was right as the image of all those cartoons came up of a man sitting over a pint of beer saying to the barman 'My wife doesn't understand me.' He never knew what the punch line would be; he was just thankful that it wasn't him in the picture.

'Yes, of course. We need to be understood. The real point is that we need to understand ourselves, and we can best do that when someone helps us to do that. And how do you get to understand someone?'

'Get to know them?' It came as a query from Adam.

'And how do you get to know them?'

3. To understand, clarify the meaning

He should have seen that one coming. Adam pondered. 'Apart from living with someone, which doesn't always work even then, I imagine, you have to find out about them. And,' he added hastily, 'that means you'd have to ask them things about themselves.'

'Indeed it does,' said Keith. 'In order to understand someone, or rather to help someone understand themselves better, we have to ask things, and the purpose of our questions is to reach greater and greater clarity. What you might see here is that, once we have heard what's important for someone, we still have to understand what that means to them. Making assumptions about what someone means and how they feel about it is the death of any helpful conversation. Instead of jumping in and declaring that you know what someone means, hold yourself back and be curious about what the other person means.'

'Let me get this straight,' murmured Adam. 'Somebody tells me something. Say when Evelyn said to me that I will need to develop a strategy, and when she talked about my having to make sacrifices and then talked about a cash flow problem, I really should have asked her what she meant. Instead, I just went away scared out of my wits and making all kinds of assumptions about what she meant.'

'Very good. Now let's go back again to the couple of conversations we had the other day. First of all, when you talked about motivation, I asked you a couple of questions about what motivated you, and then you moved on to the word "inspiration", after which I asked you some questions about what inspired you. But I not only asked you questions, I did a couple of other things to get you to a clearer understanding.' Keith leant back in his chair, his fingers pressed lightly together.

The gap gave Adam the clue that he was being asked to respond; and it also gave him a clue to what he was looking for. 'That's exactly what you did,' he exclaimed. 'You would pause and give me space to think. You did something else too, and I'm trying to think what that was.'

Keith remained silent, his head slightly tilted.

Adam obliged. 'Didn't you ask me for an example? That's right; you asked a few times, like when I talked about my wife listening to me, and how my kids give me inspiration. It was after that I realized that I enjoy being a catalyst for learning. I didn't put it like that; I said that I like to show people possibilities. I seem to recall that it was when you asked me what it feels like to be inspired and I understood that the way my kids responded to what I showed them was an inspiration to me. It's as though what inspires me is to inspire others. And that's when I decided I wanted to take that promotion.' Adam paused for breath; his words had tumbled out so fast he had had no space for breathing. 'Can I ask you a question?'

'Of course.'

'Is that what gives you inspiration; inspiring others?'

'Not exactly that. I believe that everyone has their own inspiration within them. They can't always access it, though; or they don't trust it. What inspires me, what I'm really passionate about, is empowering others to realize and act on their own inspiration.'

'I think you've done that with me already. At least I have an idea of what inspires me and what I have to do.'

'And we've only just started, Adam. E-Fitness coaching has that ability. To recap: we have looked at that third stage in Power Listening, which is to help another to understand the meaning of what they are saying, thinking and feeling by clarifying. In order to clarify, we can ask questions, we can ask for examples, we can give time for the person to reflect and we can reiterate what the other person has communicated.'

'I'm not sure you've mentioned that before,' interjected Adam.

'That's right. However, you might recall that I did some of that when we had that conversation. From time to time I simply gave back some of what you were conveying to me. And when I say that, I mean that we can go beyond the words and take note of how someone is communicating. Is someone showing excitement, anxiety, disappointment, anger or any other kind of emotion? We can pick up all those signals and begin to put the pieces together and make connections. Then, as part of this stage of clarifying what the other is presenting to us, we can offer back what we have heard and ask what it means. Do you remember that you talked about possibilities and later you talked about inspiration, and I gave you back those two words and asked if there was a connection?'

'Yes; and what's interesting is that I hadn't even remembered talking about possibilities.'

'That's exactly the purpose of a Power Listening conversation. You hear and understand things that you were unaware of even saying.'

'What,' asked Adam 'are some of the questions that you would ask?'

'Ah, that's a question that almost every coach or trainee coach asks. I'm reluctant to give you a list of great questions, because the really great question is the one that is required at the exact moment. I always take my cue from the speaker. The guideline I can give you is to ask questions that draw out further information and meaning, that help the speaker to reflect and go deeper and that take the person somewhere they may never have been. This means that the questions will challenge without judging. I seldom if ever ask questions that begin with 'Why' because that is often construed as meaning the person did something wrong. And quite often, rather than ask a question to get greater clarity, I will simply say 'Tell me more about that' or as I did with you at one point, ask the person to tell me what their own question is for themselves.'

'Pauline talks to me about intuition a lot, tells me I should use it more. What do you have to say about that?'

'Great question. The accepted wisdom is that women are much more intuitive than men and much more able to act on their intuition. In my use of Power Listening I have learned to be aware of and pick up the signals that people give out. You don't have to be a psychologist for this, and you are not expected to interpret anything. In fact, there is no interpretation or analysis going on at all in any of this E-Fitness coaching. The signals are simply the way people talk or use words, their postures and facial expressions. You know we pick these things up all the time. Think of your own little children. They tell you a lot even before they can speak. As the E-Fitness coach, your job is to concentrate on the person, not on what you are doing. When you do that, you have a much better chance of recognizing those signals and doing your best to make some connections. That's what most people call intuition, because they are usually unaware that it happens. If you like, we can call it "conscious intuition", if that's not a contradiction in terms. The term I use is "relaxed concentration", which is another apparent contradiction.'

Adam checked his watch. They had five minutes left of their agreed time. He didn't want to let this go. He could catch the train that left half an hour later, even if it were a slower one. This seemed important.

Keith noticed. 'The time has gone again. I'm all right with staying a little longer if you are. We don't have too much to get through now.

We could also take a walk through the park, which would get you nearer to the station in time to catch your train.'

'I'm fine with that. I can make a call when I'm on my way. This is more valuable to me and to Baines than my being at my desk first thing this morning. That brings up something: I'm going to talk with Evelyn about what I'm doing so that she understands that it's part of my training and preparation for my new role. So let's talk as we walk and I can take a later train if I miss my usual one.'

The park was filling up with dogs and their walkers, cyclists cutting through, men and women in business attire walking briskly, joggers running in pairs, schoolchildren dawdling in small groups. Adam and Keith strolled in a leisurely fashion, keeping to the side of the path, allowing the rest of the world to pass by as it needed.

4. To accept, summarize the essence

Keith started the conversation after they had gone a few paces. 'We've looked at how you listen by setting up the contract, hear by focusing on the issue and understand by clarifying the meaning. Now I'll talk about the fourth stage in Power Listening.'

'I'm listening,' cracked Adam, desperately trying to remember the fourth thing that Keith had told him that people needed.

Keith let him off the hook. 'You may or may not remember that the fourth need we have in our E-Fitness growth is to be and to feel accepted.'

Adam felt himself relax, only then realizing that he had tensed up in his anxiety to remember. As he had that thought, another came to him immediately on its heels. The anxiety wasn't about trying to remember; it was about being tested, being put on the spot when he wasn't ready for it. It was exactly what Keith was talking about. Adam needed to be accepted.

'Ah yes. I remember now,' was all he said.

'I know,' said Keith, 'that the conventional wisdom is that employees need to be acknowledged and rewarded in some ways other than wages to remain loyal and motivated. Acknowledgement is one thing. Being and feeling accepted are something deeper and more significant. They go to the heart of what each human being needs and open the door to our self-esteem and feeling of personal value. Now if that's not important in terms of people doing their very best, I don't know what is.'

'It's like giving respect to others so that they have it for themselves,' added Adam.

'Great connection, Adam. In our Power Listening, we have arrived at a stage where we have understood what someone is saying, or at least as best we can. To put it simply, my task now as the E-Fitness coach is to summarize the essence of what I have understood and give it back. Once again let me take you back to our conversation the other day. You had wondered what gave you inspiration and talked about your children and how you showed them possibilities, and you said that people have to respect you for you to show them possibilities. I gave you a summary of that, and I believe you added to it.'

'Yes, I said that I need to see results.'

'Thank you, yes. I seem to recall that you became very animated as well, as though you had made a great discovery and couldn't wait to do something about it.'

'That's right.' Adam stopped walking, turned to Keith. 'It was at that moment when I think I realized what my job could be all about, and that taking the next step up to sales director could be an even greater opportunity.'

They continued walking in silence for a moment.

'Let me ask you this,' said Keith. 'What do you think I was doing and how did you feel about it?'

'I'm not sure I even noticed what you were doing. I know what you didn't do: you didn't give me any advice. You were making me think about what I was saying. When you did what you said, you know, make that summary, another light went on in my head.'

'And how did you feel about what I was doing?'

'It felt like a real partnership; as though I had two thinking heads. I know that it felt safe. I knew you wouldn't cut me off or criticize what I was saying. I did feel respected and quite elated that I had discovered what inspires me.'

'With those thoughts, then, you can see that by giving you back a summary of what you had said, you felt accepted by me, which in turn gave you other positive feelings about yourself.'

They were almost at the edge of the park. Through the gate, they could see the traffic on Park Street. They hovered. Adam looked at his watch. He still had 15 minutes before the next train, and it only took him three minutes to reach the station from here. 'I have 10 minutes,' he told Keith.

'That will do it. Let's sit on this bench and I will complete this piece. Next week we will do a review and I'd like you to study the material and practise it in the meantime.'

5. To respond, move to the action

Keith started talking even before they reached the bench.

'In a way, the fifth and final phase of Power Listening has already begun by the time you have reached the stage of clarifying and summarizing the essence. You said yourself that when I summarized for you what you had said, you were already thinking about applying it in your job, and even that you'd take on that new role.

'Coaching is all about giving a response to what someone is telling you. The difference is that the response is given in a certain way, always intended to draw the wisdom from the client and to encourage them to take the action or make the changes that will bring the desired result. In Power Listening, we take account of the five needs for our emotional growth: to be listened to, to be heard, to be understood, to be accepted and to have a response. That final piece, giving a response, is as simple as asking the question "What are you going to do?" or some similar action-oriented question. It's a question that could only be answered at this time, which means that the skill of the coach is in knowing when that time is. When I asked you the other day what you wanted to do with the information that you now had, you already had the answer rolling out of you. How different is that from my telling you to take the job?'

'It would probably have scared me too much. Once I saw my whole purpose in a different light, it seemed the perfect fit for me all of a sudden. I really like the way it happened, as though the answer just came to me. If I can do what you did for others it will be exactly what inspires me.'

'Well,' replied Keith, 'you don't have to wait. You can try it out this week and we can talk about it next time. Here's the quick reminder of the Power Listening stages for you to take in. And don't forget to keep out of the way when you practise.'

Framework for Power Listening

In Figure 2.1 you will find the framework that Keith gave to Adam. While the framework is a simple one, it is deceptively simple to use.

FIGURE 2.1   Power Listening

Power Listening

1. In order to *listen* or be listened to
   .... *establish* a *contract*.

2. In order to *hear* what someone is saying
   ....….. *focus* on what they want to say.

3. In order to *understand* what the person is saying
   …….....…............... *clarify* what is being presented.

4. In order to *accept* someone and what they say
   ....*summarize* the
   essence of what you have understood.

5. In order to *respond* to the person
   .... help them towards their own
   appropriate *action*.

Remember: keep yourself out of the way

Your challenge is to practise Power Listening. If you are already a coach, you are in a good position to work with someone using the framework described here. Otherwise, consider which two or three people you could try out Power Listening with over the next few days.

It will be of help to you to read over the chapter again and visualize whom you might work with.

After each practice session, write down your own notes on how the conversation went, and in particular how you fared using the framework of Power Listening. Remember to record what your 'client' or employee wanted to achieve from the conversation and what the result was. Take the opportunity to check back with the person later to ask for feedback and what action has been taken. Note whenever there has been a change in relation to the person's work that has an impact on anyone else or on the person's productivity. Don't expect to get it perfect first time; but do expect something extraordinary to happen.

The test

Adam didn't have to wait long. As he arrived at the plant, Claudia, the receptionist, greeted him with a 'Good morning' through rather pursed lips and the information that Mr Baines wanted to see him when he got in. He went into his own office first, noticing his heart beating. A note from Andrea, Marcus Baines's assistant, sat on Adam's desk. Andrea believed in writing notes rather than trusting too much to the computer. What could the boss want with him?

'Ah, Adam.' Marcus stood up to greet Adam as he came through the door. 'Shut the door and come and sit down. Evelyn tells me that you have accepted this job of hers when she steps up to take over from me. Very pleased. Very pleased indeed, and I'm sure you'll do a wonderful job. Congratulations.'

'Thank you, Mr Baines. It's a great honour and I can assure you I will do my best.' Adam blushed. Thoughts whirled. Is that it? Strange that Evelyn isn't here. Am I supposed to say something else?

Marcus nodded. 'Now I know that Evelyn will handle this, but I just wanted to say a couple of things to you, Adam.'

Adam noticed two things. The first was that he became wary, waiting for some bombshell to drop. The second was that he noticed that he noticed, and he remembered his lessons from Keith.

Marcus Baines sat back in his chair and gave a sigh. 'This is between you and me,' he said conspiratorially.

'Absolutely, Mr Baines. I'll keep this entirely confidential as you wish. My time is yours. What would you like to say?' A part of Adam's mind congratulated himself for getting out of the way, setting up a contract and asking Marcus what he'd like to focus on, all in the same sentence. Another part wondered if he wasn't going too fast. He stopped himself, reminded himself to relax and concentrate.

Marcus shifted a little in his seat. 'I started this company with my brother 46 years ago. I was only 21. When he died only two years later I never imagined I could carry on, much less make a success of the business. But here we are. It's been my life, you know. Well, I'm ready to move on and I'm happy that my niece is taking over the helm. It keeps it in the family, and Evelyn is also a very competent and experienced manager. But it takes a lot to run a company. I had to learn the hard way and of course it grew gradually. Now we have over 1,500 employees and sales nearing £50 million this year. I never dreamed of that. Being sales director is a big job and you have six months to get into it, just as Evelyn has six months before she takes over the reins.' He paused.

'Are you concerned about that, sir?'

'Well, of course I want to make sure that the business is in the right hands. We have a good management team. It's just that you and Evelyn are, in a way, the newcomers to the team in big roles and some of the others have been around for a while and may feel a bit put out. That's going to be Evelyn's job to handle, but you will also be taking over the sales team where you may be seen as leapfrogging over a few others.'

'As I understand it,' said Adam, 'you see a possible problem in our being accepted by the team. Is that right?'

'Exactly so. Glad you see that. I also want to see our overseas sales take off in the next couple of years.'

'Yes, Evelyn spoke with me about that. What do you see as your own role after the next six months?' Adam felt his forehead and cheeks get warm as he asked the question. He was about to add something, anything that might soften the edge to what he had just asked; decided against it. 'See what happens,' he thought, still feeling the heat curling around his body.

This time Marcus sat up straight in the chair, eyed Adam curiously. 'My role? I'm going to retire. Take time with my wife. Travel. That sort of thing. But that doesn't mean I won't have an interest in the business. My role?' He sat silently, took his eyes away from Adam and gazed out of the window. 'That's a very good question. I can see I shall have to think about this.'

'I don't quite understand, if you don't mind my saying so. You mentioned that you were ready to move on and happy that Evelyn was taking over. You are obviously very proud of how the business has grown over the years and that it's been your life. You want to be sure that the business is in good hands and that it expands, especially in overseas sales. You have some concern that Evelyn and I may have a little difficulty in being accepted. And you are wondering what role, if any, you might have in the future.'

There was a long silence. Adam wondered if he was about to lose his job. He dragged himself from his own negative thoughts to concentrate on Marcus.

The owner of Baines Electronics stroked his chin. 'You've given me some food for thought, young man. I must discuss this with Evelyn, but I think I've had in my mind that I would continue to pop into the place a couple of days a week without any clear idea what I'd be doing. It's hard to let go after all this time.'

'I can certainly understand that. Is there anything you would like me to do, sir?'

'You? Apart from preparing for your job and finding a replacement for your current one, I don't think so. But if I had any doubts about your abilities before, I certainly don't now.'

'Thank you, Mr Baines.' Adam swallowed hard. 'And is there anything that you want to do from this conversation?'

'As I said, I shall talk to Evelyn. But you've made me think that I should ask her what she wants from me. I can see that she might not want me to interfere. Perhaps she could use me as a kind of consultant. Come to that, you might find some of my contacts useful. I'll see who I should introduce you to.'

Back in his office, Adam reflected that Keith hadn't mentioned to him a quality needed in an E-Fitness coach. 'Courage,' he thought. 'You need courage to do this; especially when your client is actually the boss of the company you work for.'

Learning is earning

How Learning from Experience brings wealth to everyone

The files of the 42 UK sales people sat on Adam's desk, neatly stacked into the four regions they represented. While he was familiar with the 11 sales reps that were his colleagues in the Midlands and Wales and whom he now managed, Adam wanted to know more about the others. After all, it was highly likely that his successor would be drawn from one of them, just as he had been. He planned to advertise the position when the time was right, but before that he wanted to get a feel of who might be right and who he'd like to have in this seat. He wanted to make sure that he didn't give preference to someone from his own team, even though his gut feeling kept going towards Max.

Max was a natural. He was personable, knowledgeable and loyal. Above all, he was passionate about selling and seemed to love the products and the customers he served. His figures were good, although not great. If only he didn't have this habit of accepting contracts for custom-made equipment and giving unrealistic delivery dates to the clients. That's what their argument had been about the other day. Max was so keen to satisfy his customers that he caused mayhem in the plant, leaving his manager (Adam in this case) to fight it out with the production supervisor and his boss, the operations director, Sam Chandler. Sam: now there was someone he'd have to deal with more often in the future. For the hundredth time or more, Adam wondered whether he was up to this task.

The roots of Learning from Experience

'Why is it that some people never seem to learn?' Adam leaned into his opening question almost aggressively, challenging Keith to answer this one.

'What's sparked that?' asked Keith, totally unmoved by Adam's body language.

'Oh, just me feeling in the middle, I suppose. You remember Sam Chandler, of course. As you know, he's been at Baines for ever and he's pretty set in his ways. He doesn't know it yet, but when I step up as sales director, he and I are going to be working together closely. Sam's a great guy, except that he has no time for salespeople, whom he seems to regard as parasites. He sees them as producing nothing and earning a lot for doing it. He regards any requests out of the ordinary, like design differences or requests for specials or quick de-livery times as being a pain in the ... well, a real nuisance, and then he gets obstructive and argumentative. On the other hand, there's Max, one of those salespeople, who goes out of his way to help the customer and puts what appear to be unreasonable demands on the production side. Max isn't the only one, of course, but it happened again this week. Neither of them learns; they both keep acting out the same way. It doesn't make life easy for me and it's going to get worse if I don't know how to handle it.'

'Now,' said Keith, 'I will answer your question. As it happens, you have led right into the second tool of E-Fitness coaching: Learning from Experience. It was actually developed in the nineties by Warren Redman, who wrote about it in a book called *Portfolios for Development*. Briefly, it started when Redman was engaged by a government department to examine ways in which people could gain credits for their experience rather than have to take training in order to become qualified. It was called the Portfolio Approach and showed how we can demonstrate competencies that are required for certain jobs. The interesting thing, and how it became integrated into E-Fitness, was that the very process of asking people to reflect on their experience provided them with new insights about themselves and raised their levels of self-esteem, confidence and creative awareness.'

'We could do with more of that,' commented Adam. 'It still doesn't answer my question about why people don't seem to learn, though.'

Keith smiled. 'The simple answer to that is, nobody asks them what they know and nobody uses Power Listening to help them to find out about themselves.'

Adult learning: why most training doesn't work

'There are many theories about different learning styles and how adults learn,' continued Keith. 'All I want to say here is that, while each of us has different capacities for learning, all of us are able to absorb amazing amounts of information from very earliest ages. Just think about your children and that Mark has managed to learn a whole language, or the best part of it, by the age of four. And you didn't even teach him. Your two-year-old is learning just the same right now, she is just not quite articulating everything she has in her head yet. We do know that as we get older, our capacity for learning becomes less; but it's still enormous. What's really important to understand, as far as our emotional learning is concerned, is that we have learned the best part of it by the time we are four or five. Psychologists in the sixties showed very clearly that by that age we are almost completely formed in terms of our psychological make-up. More recently, psychologists have shown that our emotional being is already wired in at birth: part of the genetic make-up that we inherited in order to survive.'

'Do you mean to say,' asked Adam incredulously, 'that we can't change who we are? I'm glad that's so for Mark – he's such a bright and happy child. So he'll always be that way? And does it also mean that someone like Sam is always going to be difficult with people who aren't like him and whom he distrusts?'

'I would say,' said Keith, 'that Mark is likely to have those characteristics always at his core. It doesn't mean that when he's an adolescent he won't go through the usual trying times, or that if something bad happened to him he wouldn't become cautious or unhappy. But I do believe that these would be temporary states for him and that he will always get back to who he really is, sometimes with help from others who could help him understand that. As for Sam Chandler and millions of others like him; who knows what experiences have helped to cover or inhibit who he really is?

'What it indicates, though, is how hard it is, for adults especially, to learn to change how they feel and how they behave in given circumstances. While we may be able to take in information, to a greater or lesser extent, depending on our abilities and learning styles, we are unlikely to learn to make changes that have an impact upon our emotional being. For example, Sam won't learn to change his behaviour because you show him it doesn't work. He'll only change it when he gets it for himself and when there is some emotional payoff for him.

'That's why so much training doesn't actually work in terms of people changing their behaviour. Training is good for giving information about technical things, although you could always get that from a book or the internet. But most training that purports to improve motivation or how people communicate, or to help them improve self-awareness and so on, doesn't work because it mainly deals with our cognitive, our logical, thinking selves, ignoring the fact that almost everybody already knows what they should be doing but have emotional blockages that disable them from doing it.'

The penalties of not learning from experience

'Sounds a bit gloomy to me,' remarked Adam. 'I hope you're going to show me how to get around this. If I'm to show people possibilities, and want them to act on them, I'd better have something that works. I have an inkling into why people don't learn. Now I want to know how to get them to learn. I mean, it must be hugely expensive if we continue to make the same mistakes, or if we don't learn how to do things better.'

'Yes, it is. We talked about the mistakes that led to the Clapham train crash and the space mission disaster, but there are millions of errors that take place that are very costly and are due to people not learning from their own previous experience. I told you when we first met in the park about Peter, the man who told me about E-Fitness. His company had won awards in training and yet he told me that nobody learned anything; they kept repeating the same mistakes. Those mistakes, each one not apparently significant in itself, added up to such a whopping amount in lost revenue or wastage that the firm was on the edge of bankruptcy.

'Then there was the footwear company I did some work with. They manufactured shoes for some of the biggest retail outlets in the country. Their quality control was poor and they consistently had huge amounts of returns until they too nearly went broke. Nobody, not the designers, the operatives, the supervisors or the managers, seemed to notice the failures of communication that contributed to tiny errors, causing shoddy results. Everybody kept blaming everybody else. If that kind of culture continued it would have closed the factory, putting thousands of people out of work. Sadly, that seems to be the working norm in far too many businesses.'

The excuses for not learning

'I don't think we're that bad at Baines Electronics,' said Adam, rather defensively he thought, knowing that Keith had worked there for 22 years. 'I know that we could improve a lot, though,' he added quickly. 'It's mostly down to time. Everyone is so busy doing the stuff they are supposed to be doing, there is no time for learning how to do it better.'

'That,' said Keith, 'is the main excuse given. In the end, those businesses I told you about almost ran out of time altogether. What other excuses come up?'

'Apart from not wanting to invest the time, there's usually an unwillingness to invest money in this sort of thing. It's usually easy to persuade the managers at Baines to pay out money for technical or safety training and for things that have some obvious benefits. But I can't see anyone there saying "Let's pay for some training in how to listen." So, time and money are the main ones. I'd say that those might be the excuses given, but I can see that the real reason is that people don't want to admit to having shortcomings in the kind of things we're talking about. I mean, it's much easier to say that I need upgrading in something technical, or some sales training. It's harder to say that I don't communicate well. Nobody wants to think that.'

'You're still talking about training, Adam. What if we were able to deal with all three of those barriers – time, money and personal reticence – through some E-Fitness coaching?'

'Now you're talking, Keith.'

'Let's try something out, then. My aim here is to show you how easy it is to learn, starting with an everyday occurrence.'

'I'm ready for anything. Would you like another coffee? I'm ready for one of those too.'

The young woman who was their regular server had already anticipated their readiness and was walking towards them, coffee jug in hand.

Make it easy to learn

Keith took a sip, put down his mug, and inclined his head in that manner that Adam had come to expect when he was about to ask a question. 'Tell me, Adam, about something that you experienced or noticed at work in the last day or two.'

'Oh, well. Plenty of things. You want just one? Let me see. I could just continue with what I mentioned before, the conversations I had with Max and then with Sam. More of a confrontation, really.'

'Okay, describe what happened.'

'First I have this order come in from Max. It was from a regular customer of his, not a big client but steady. They mostly supply organizations like community halls with their sound equipment and so on. Anyway, they wanted a range of speakers and audio players for a big event that is coming up in the autumn and they have their own specification requirements that mean we would have to treat it as a special order, which always takes longer and is more expensive to produce, as you know. I called Max and told him that the delivery date was really tight, and that the price he quoted didn't reflect the additional work. I asked him to go back to the customer to explain this, and that we needed to add 10 per cent. He was really unhappy, and refused. He has a point but I just knew what Sam and Evelyn would say. Then I took the order to Sam, who looked at it and said "Can't be done; we've already got a full schedule for autumn and I can't take on specials at this point." He wouldn't budge and suggested I talk to Evelyn. He would have said Mr Baines, but he's just started to accept Evelyn as sales director. I spoke to Evelyn and she basically told me to deal with it. Finally I went back to Sam and asked if we could make some adjustments. I knew there was one order that could be split in two, with one part delivered later. As it happens, it was one of my customers. Then I pleaded with him and said how grateful we'd all be. I know he likes that. Eventually, and reluctantly, he agreed to fit it in. Lastly I called Max and told him what a time waster this had all been and please not to do this again.'

Keith nodded as Adam finished his story. 'What I understand from this is that you were in between one person making unreasonable demands and another refusing to budge, and a third not willing to take part. You found a compromise and told the originator of the problem not to do it again. Is that right?'

'Yes, that's about it.'

'Now tell me,' said Keith, 'what you have learned from this experience.'

'I learned that some people are just not reasonable.'

'And ... ?' queried Keith.

'I can find a compromise. I get quite flustered and run around trying to fix things. I can think of ways to make it work. I get angry with people who take things for granted. I can figure out how to get around people like Sam. Wow – I think I learned a lot, now I think about it. Mostly about myself.'

'That's an excellent list to start with. You may find some more things. Meanwhile, let's take the most important piece of learning. What do you think that was?'

Adam thought for a moment. 'I'd say the fact that I can find compromises, together with being able to come up with ideas of how to make something work. That's two things really.'

'Can you put them together to make them one?'

'I'm able to suggest a new way of looking at something so that I can find a compromise that works for people. Now that I say it, I see that it's not so much a compromise; it's a way for me to negotiate a solution.'

'Good. You've told me what happened. Now you have told me some of the things that you learned and you have selected one of those, which is that you come up with new ways of looking at a problem that help you negotiate and find solutions.'

Adam expelled a deep breath. 'Yes.'

'Now then,' continued Keith, 'I'd like you to give me a different example of how you do that. Where else have you come up with an idea that helped you to negotiate through a problem?'

Adam's hand went up to his chin. He furrowed his brow, scratched his forehead and looked at Keith, his eyes suddenly wide open. 'I know. We had a meeting of the sales team a couple of months ago. Evelyn was chairing it. There was an issue about a new product we had just brought to the market to replace an older item and quite a few of the sales reps were complaining that it didn't have some of the features that the old one had. I piped up that the new one had some seriously good benefits and that if customers wanted the other features we still had stocks of a previous model that we hadn't been using for a while. It seemed to satisfy everyone. You know, I do think that Evelyn asked me to take on the regional manager's job partly because of how she saw me there, although that wasn't my reason.'

'Great example, Adam. Can you think of another?'

'Let's see. Well, I had this conversation with Evelyn just yesterday. I wanted to talk to her about overseas sales, since that's a big part of our strategy in the next year. Marcus Baines had always wanted this to expand and he'd appointed some people as our agents in North America and a few in Western and Eastern European cities. Marcus likes the personal touch and I know his idea was to find more overseas agents. I asked Evelyn how she wanted to proceed and she seemed to be thinking the same way. I suggested that we investigate marketing and selling through the internet, aiming at specific markets in different countries. She liked the idea and asked me to follow it up and come back with a proposal and budget. It's odd, given our business, that neither Marcus nor Evelyn are fans of technology in marketing; but I think I gave her a persuasive argument in favour of us going in that direction.'

'Well, thank you, Adam; you've given me two more examples of how you do indeed demonstrate that you have those particular strengths: the ability to come up with creative ideas to produce solutions.'

'You know, I hadn't quite seen that. I suppose I do.'

'Now,' said Keith, 'remembering back to those other things you learned, like getting flustered and getting angry with people who take things for granted, what else do you think you need to learn in order to be more successful and more emotionally fit?'

'That's easy. Not to get flustered or angry. Easier said than done.'

'Tell me more about getting flustered.'

'It's when those situations occur, especially when I feel I'm in the middle. Actually, that's exactly it. When I feel put into the position of kind of refereeing when others are arguing, I tend to feel an obligation to put it right and I don't think I know if I can.' Adam paused. There was a silence, broken by Adam with another deep sigh. 'I know exactly where that comes from,' he said.

'I thought you would,' Keith remarked. 'While that's something you might care to explore at some time, I want you to hold that thought while I ask you the next question. In relation to feeling flustered, how are you going to learn to change that?'

'I wish I knew.'

'Let me summarize what you have told me, Adam. You come up with creative ideas to achieve solutions with people. You get flustered when you feel in the middle because you don't know if you can put it right, and you know where that feeling comes from.'

The light that had been flickering in Adam's head lit up brilliantly. He couldn't get used to this sensation, although it was beginning to occur regularly.

'I do know,' he almost shouted, and he noticed several heads at adjoining tables turn in his direction. He dropped his voice. 'When I get flustered I can tell myself two things. The first is that I do come up with good ideas; they never let me down. I have to trust myself. The other thing is that I have to remember that I'm not a kid any more in the middle of two arguing parents.'

'And that,' smiled Keith, leaning back, 'is Learning from Experience.'

Same as usual

Sam Chandler looked down from his office perch above the assembly floor. He watched as Marcus Baines made his way past the rows of stations, smiling and chatting with some of the operatives. It was the eight o'clock ritual. Marcus climbed the steps.

'Good morning, Sam.'

'Good morning Mr Baines.' Sam had known Marcus since starting at Baines Electronics as a young man. Now he was 48, had worked his way up to be operations director and still only ever addressed his boss as 'Mr Baines'.

Marcus closed the door from the noise of the plant below. 'How's that new lapel microphone set coming along?'

Sam crinkled his face. 'I tried out the second prototype yesterday, Mr Baines. It's not there yet. The switch on the receiver isn't stable and the lapel clip is very awkward to use. I don't know whether it's the design or the materials we're using or just careless work, but this is the third or fourth time in the past couple of months that we've come up with a good idea and it takes for ever to get the thing right.'

'What have you done about it, Sam?' asked Marcus.

'Same as usual. I shove it back to them and tell them to get it right. At least it's not gone into production, like that load of audio recorders we put out and the cue mode didn't work. I don't know how much time and money we lost through that, but it makes me wild when things get through like that. It's why I insist on testing every prototype personally now. Just can't trust some of these testers.'

'Ah well, you'll work it out, Sam. I can always rely on you. Why don't you have a word with Evelyn about it?'

Sam looked at Marcus with a frown. 'Why should I do that? She's sales. She knows nothing about electronics.' He hesitated, seeing the expression on Marcus's face. 'But if you think I should, of course I will.'

The model

Keith pulled out a folder from his briefcase, handed it to Adam and pointed to the diagram on the front. 'That's what we've just done,' he said. 'This is the Learning from Experience model. You'll notice that I still used Power Listening, but in a specific way, structured to allow you to see what you learn as you go along.'

'It didn't only do that,' said Adam, 'It also made me think what makes me feel stuck and how I can change that.'

'Let's see what happened,' Keith said. Take a look at this model.

'First I asked you to talk about a specific experience that you had recently. That's your story. I listened, clarified a few things, and summarized back to you. Next I asked what you had learned from the experience. That's your discovery; and it seems that you discovered some very significant things about yourself in the process.'

'I certainly did,' agreed Adam, nodding his head vigorously.

'After you told me what you learned, I asked for other examples of how you demonstrate those qualities. You gave me two others. That's your proof that you not only learn those things, but you also behave

FIGURE 3.1   The Learning from Experience model

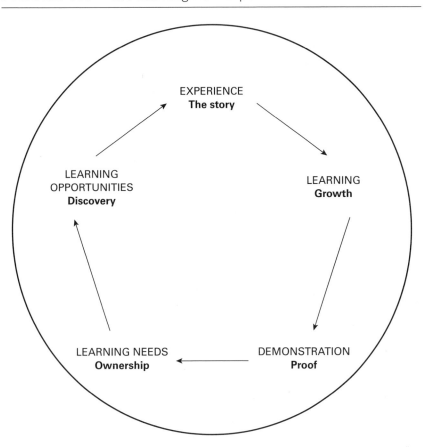

that way. Notice that we only examined two of your tendencies which, with further thought, you put into one: that you have the ability to come up with good ideas that help you to negotiate solutions. Those are strengths. It's important that you acknowledge and value your strengths so that you are able to capitalize on them.

'Next, I asked you to consider what you still needed to learn in the kind of situation you described. You told me that you wanted to stop getting angry and frustrated. Because it was you who declared them, not me, this is you taking ownership of your learning needs. That's why we call that piece "ownership". When people take ownership of what they need to learn, they are much more likely to want to learn it. Finally, I asked you how you were going to learn to deal with your frustration in a healthier way. You were a little stuck on that, until

I summarized back to you again what you had said, at which time you became quite enthusiastic and told me what you would do in the future. That is your growth point.'

Adam stared at the diagram, following the steps and his own progress through them. 'It feels, in a way,' he reflected, 'that I did grow up.'

'The real test is about to come,' said Keith, smiling broadly at him. You have declared what you are going to do. Now you have to do it. I'll expect you to tell me about that next time. Meanwhile, I suggest that you jot down what you talked about today. I'll give you the outline and you can fill in the details. It will also remind you of the five stages of Learning from Experience.'

On the train, Adam jotted down the notes from the coaching conversation.

The five stages of Learning from Experience

1 The story: describing experience. Pick something that is specific and that you would like to change or improve upon.

2 Discovery: what was learned. Ask yourself the question 'What did I learn from this?' Write down both positive and negative things.

3 Proof: demonstrating how the learning is used now. Think of other examples, more recent or earlier, that show how you reinforce what you learn in your actions.

4 Ownership: accepting what still needs to be learned. Consider and decide what you want to learn that will improve how you act in the future.

5 Growth: taking up new learning opportunities. Decide how you will learn this and make a learning plan. Practise what you learn and take this forward to a new experience. That will be your measurement of success.

He read it back to himself and looked at the folder that Keith had given him. He started to fill in the spaces with the experience he had described. As he wrote, it seemed that he was reliving the experience and gaining more understanding of his own strengths and how he could change those things that didn't work for him.

The story

Description of one experience.
Select a specific event or experience. Describe this experience to
a listener or Emotional Fitness coach if you have one.
Write down a summary of what you have said:

Discovery

What I have learned from that experience.
Next, read back what you have written in your story and explore, with
the help of your listener, what you now understand that you have learned
from the experience.
When you are ready, write down what you have learned (discovered about
yourself):

Proof

How I demonstrate that I use what I learned.

Discuss how you now use what you have learned from the experience just described. How can you demonstrate what you learned? Be creative and give examples to show what you know and can do and believe.

Write down your examples. These are (or will become) your strengths:

Ownership

What else I need to learn.

Talk with your listener about what else you need to learn in this area and summarize this for yourself.

Write down your summary:

Growth

What learning opportunities I plan to take up.
Finally, look at how you want to learn and what opportunities you want to carve out for yourself. Do you prefer to read things, practise them, go on courses, ask somebody, or what? Give yourself a realistic time for you to carry out your plan.
Write down your plan here:

At a later date (note the date now that you intend to do this), add notes to show that you have carried out your plan and the results you have achieved.

Reluctant learner

Adam put his head around Evelyn's door, which was slightly ajar. He was surprised to see Sam sitting at the small informal table with Evelyn next to him. 'Sorry,' murmured Adam and, just about to withdraw his head, was arrested in that movement by Evelyn's hearty cry.

'Just the person,' she called. 'Come on in, Adam.'

Once Adam had seated himself at the table, Evelyn launched into an explanation. 'Sam here has a few things he wanted to discuss and one of them was how we sometimes throw special orders at him with too short a delivery date. Since one of the offenders is your man Max, I thought it was opportune that you were around.' She looked sharply at Adam. 'I was also going to tell Sam about the changes that are taking place.'

Sam shifted uncomfortably in the chair that was a little too small for his build. 'What changes are those, then?' he asked, bouncing his gaze from one to the other.

'This has to be kept confidential, Sam. I discussed it with Marcus and he agrees you should know; but the three of us here are the only ones. Marcus is going to retire in just over five months and I will be taking over. Adam will be stepping up into my place. You, Sam will of course remain as operations director. So you see, it is important that you and Adam have good communication between the two of you. As it happens, we have a perfect example of the things that you will have to resolve. Frankly, I don't want to get involved in such issues. I'd rather management team members sort out any internal concerns. I'm going to have my work cut out learning about the running of this business.'

Sam sat with his mouth open. Adam, his head still catching up with this conversation, saw in it the opportunity that he was hoping to carve out being offered to him on a plate.

'Frankly, I'm very relieved and pleased that Sam knows. He's the most important and valuable person we have and the one who's been with Baines the longest. It gives us a head start too. You might have a lot to learn Evelyn, but so do we all. I do, of course, but I would like to see that everyone in the company really does learn from the experience that we all have. This thing about the special orders, for example, has been going on for as long as I can remember and always causes some difficulty, and often something goes wrong as a result.'

'Very simple, as I see it.' Sam seemed to have regained his composure as well as some of his belligerence. 'Just tell the sales people not to take specials without giving an extra two months for delivery or checking with me first.'

'It's probably not as simple as it sounds, Sam,' countered Evelyn. 'What were you getting at, Adam? What do you have in mind?'

'I only used the special orders as an example, since you mentioned it as a problem. My point is that we could be much more cost effective and efficient, and serve our customers much better, if we paid more attention to the things that go wrong and learn from them instead of passing blame around.'

'I wasn't blaming anyone,' grumbled Sam. 'And who's saying we're not efficient? I run the shop floor the best I can with what I have. Can't always get the staff; but we still get the stuff out to specification and on time 90 per cent of the time. Probably 95 per cent.'

Adam and Evelyn exchanged glances. Adam spoke first. 'I met someone recently who has been coaching me and he told me about a company that saved millions by asking employees what they had learned from their everyday experience at work. I'm sure we could do the same. Well, maybe not millions – we're not so big – but it would be significant. And the thing is, when he described it to me, it's really simple. We don't need any big consulting firm to come in and tell us how to run things; we already know, as Sam says. What we can do better, though, is to make sure that we don't repeat mistakes, and that we learn from the good and the not-so-good things we do.'

Sam shifted in his chair again. 'Sounds like all we have to do is use our common sense. If everyone did that we'd have no problems at all.'

'True enough, Sam,' said Adam. 'We also know that common sense isn't so common. What I'm talking about is how to make it a lot more common. All we have to do is to get people to think about what they have been doing.'

'And how are you going to do that?' Evelyn and Sam spoke the same words at the same time. Only the tone was different.

'The best way for me to explain it is to try it out. Are you open to that? It will take about 10 minutes.'

'Go for it, Adam,' said Evelyn, while Sam shrugged his shoulders and gave what could have been construed as a nod.

An image of Keith fluttered across Adam's consciousness as he heard the words 'relax and concentrate' and tried to dispel the anxiety that was beginning to creep in. 'Tell you what,' he said, smiling directly at Sam, 'why don't I try it out on you?'

Before Sam could respond, Evelyn chipped in. 'Great idea; I can watch and learn.'

Adam wondered if Sam would think there was some kind of conspiracy going on and decided to ignore the thought.

'This is a great example of how we can collaborate,' said Adam, noticing his diplomatic ability. 'Now Sam, can you give me an example of something that has happened recently that you'd like to change? Maybe you want to talk about the special orders.'

'No, I don't think so.' Sam spoke slowly; reluctantly.

'What then?' asked Adam.

Sam looked at Evelyn. There was a silence. Adam willed Evelyn not to say anything. She came up trumps. Sam succumbed.

'Well,' he drawled. 'As I was saying to Evelyn earlier; we have a bit of a problem with the new lapel mike set that was supposed to be a bit of a design breakthrough. I tested it out yesterday for the second time and there are still faults with it. I just can't understand how the testers can let it through, or where the problems originate. It's a design fault, bad material, shoddy work or poor inspection; or something of everything.'

'What have you done so far, Sam?'

'Same as I always do: chuck it back to them and tell them to get it right. I don't have time to go through every little detail. It's bad enough having to do a final test myself now.'

'What do you mean?'

'Well, it's happened so often that a product supposedly ready for production has a glitch in it that I insisted on them bringing every prototype to me before we start making them. We have testers for that, but as I said before, it's hard to find good staff.'

'What's the result of all this?'

'Apart from it being a waste of my time? Well, we're paying two or three times for people doing the same thing. It holds up other new products being tested. Sometimes, like when we put that lot of faulty audio recorders out, it costs a lot in overtime to fix it, plus all the waste of material. And I suppose the customer couldn't have been very pleased. I know Mr Baines wasn't.'

'So if you could change this, you and lots of other people would be pleased.'

'You could say that, yes.'

'So, Sam, if I understand this properly, you have taken to testing prototypes because you can't trust the testers, and you discover that this last one is still faulty after the second time. Your action is to send it back to them and tell them to get it right. Who is "them" by the way?' Adam kicked himself mentally for not asking that before.

'Them? Oh, I mean the project supervisor.'

'Right. Anyway, if that's how it was, could you tell me what you have learned from this experience so far?'

'Learned?'

Adam bit down on his lower lip, now willing himself to say nothing except the one word. 'Yes.'

Sam looked around for help, but Evelyn had her head down and there was nobody else to come to the rescue.

'I learned that you can't trust people to get it right. If you want something doing well, do it yourself.' He leant back smugly.

'What else did you learn?' insisted Adam.

Sam seemed to want to escape now, gazing at the door to his right. 'I don't know.'

Evelyn could stay silent no longer. 'Have a go, Sam. Adam's trying something here and needs our cooperation.'

Sam's face went red, his eyes squinted and his mouth tightened; then almost as quickly as he tensed, he began to relax. He even managed a smile.

'Well, as my wife tells me, I'm an impatient bugger sometimes.' And the three of them laughed.

Just over eight minutes later, with Adam's encouragement and new-found skills, Sam had described what he had learned, how he regularly demonstrated both the positive and negative sides of his behaviour, what he needed to learn and what learning action he was going to take.

Adam summarized it back to him. 'You learned from the experience of rejecting the faulty prototype a few things, Sam. You learned that it's hard for you to trust others to do things as well as you'd like and that when you become impatient, you take on things that aren't yours to do. You have also told us that you are a perfectionist, have an intense loyalty to Baines and that you prefer getting your hands dirty to managing others. You gave a couple of examples of how this shows itself up regularly. What you said you wanted to learn is how to be more patient and at the same time improve quality and that you want to get more comfortable managing others. The action you came up with is to ask your project supervisor how to improve the process and you will read that book on leadership that you've had on your desk for several months.'

Sam put on his glum expression. 'That's about it, yes.'

'That's very interesting, Adam,' said Evelyn as they stood up. 'I'd like to have a conversation about this with you. And Sam, I really appreciate you putting yourself on the hot seat for this. Let me know if you'd like some help; I'd be glad to talk about the book with you.'

'No, that's fine, thanks. I'll manage.' Sam was edging out of the office.

'Actually,' Adam chimed in, 'I suggest that we get together in a week to go over this again and see how Sam has done. We'd have a lot to learn from what happens; and if we really would like people to learn and improve our working practices, we ought to try it out ourselves for a while. Let's see the results.'

'Good idea,' said Evelyn. 'Since we are the only ones apart from Marcus who know about the changes, we should meet on a regular basis anyway to get to know each other better. We have a lot to learn from you, Sam, and I need to get up to speed with the operating side.'

Results

'I have a lot to tell you,' said Adam before they had even sat down. It was two weeks later and they were at their regular table at the Corner Café. 'By the way, how was your break?'

'It was excellent,' said Keith. 'I was at a coaching conference and helped to run a workshop on E-Fitness coaching. My co-facilitator was Peter, who talked about the phenomenal benefits that his company reaped after instituting some E-Fitness coaching practices. There were some very tangible rewards so that they could measure their ROI. The financial gains through lower staff turnover, decreased wastage, improved performance and even higher sales added up to millions over the year. What was less measurable, but equally important and visible in many ways, was the difference it made to employees at all levels. When they felt listened to and found that their contributions were acknowledged, they became more motivated, more confident and communicative. Of course, those were the intangible changes, the emotional ones if you like, that caused the bottom line to improve. Very exciting stuff.'

'Can you give an example of how it happened?' asked Adam.

'Peter gave a few. People were asked to record something they had seen or experienced and to report this to their line manager. Remember, this was a firm of catering contractors, so some of the managers were chefs, some were sales executives like you. All the managers had received some training and preparation in E-Fitness coaching – enough to help them to use the formats that were provided. Anyway, there are two examples that I recall. One was at the executive level, when a regional manager told her boss that on her way to work she had noticed a high-rise office building that had just been purchased by a major company after being vacant for a year. When her boss asked what she had learned from this, she told him that it looked like an opportunity for a catering contractor. To cut a long story short, she passed the message on to the sales team, who eventually obtained the contract.

'Another was a smaller example, which had a lot of cost-cutting consequences when a kitchen employee mentioned the coffee machines that created a lot of spillage. They brought in a mechanic from the coffee company and made a minor adjustment. They worked out that they saved about £1 a day for each machine. With over 5,000 coffee machines being used around the country, that's £1,500,000 a year, not to mention the time it took to clear the mess and the disgruntled customers. The employee had her picture taken for the company magazine when she was given the award for good idea of the month, instituted directly from the E-Fitness pro-gramme. Now give me your news, Adam.'

'Well, I'm not sure we can match that yet. There has been some progress, though. I sat with Sam and Evelyn and went through Learning from Experience with Sam. I honestly thought it was going nowhere; in fact, I felt I might have ruined a chance of persuading Evelyn that Emotional Fitness coaching was a good idea. At first Sam was pretty negative and defensive. Then at the end, after he'd agreed what he would do, it seemed like he was just trying to get out of the room and get on with his work as usual.' Adam's voice rose, his eyes brightened. 'We'd agreed to meet again, thanks to Evelyn supporting the idea, and it was incredible. Sam was a different man.'

'Now this sounds intriguing. If you managed to turn Sam around you must have done a tremendous job. He's a very good person, but he can be pretty stubborn.'

'Yes. Well, anyway, he came into the office looking his usual mournful self; then he recounted what had happened. He'd been having problems with a new piece of equipment and said that he'd spoken with the supervisor, as agreed, and actually seemed to have listened to him. He told us that the supervisor had lots to say and explained where he thought things had gone wrong. Sam said that he'd read about being a good leader and realized that he hadn't been giving his staff enough of a say in their own work. Anyway, they both went along and talked with the designer and testers. As a result they found the glitches. Sam was happy with the last prototype, which can go into production now. By the end he couldn't contain his glee when he told us that he thought he had really discovered something about being a good manager and had enjoyed it. He admitted to always being in awe of Mr Baines and that he didn't think he could live up to his expectations. He even said at the end that he'd been shocked when he heard that Evelyn was going to be the boss and I would be in charge of sales for the company, but that this had given him "a new lease on life", as he put it.'

Keith nodded slowly. 'You're a brilliant learner, Adam. You can chalk this up to another experience; then you can go through the whole process again using that experience, and say what you have learned from it. That's the way learning becomes continuous, and continuous learning is synonymous with progress. And progress in business is synonymous with improved earnings. So learning really is earning. And next time we will take a look at how you can take this forward to teams, where there is some buried treasure waiting to be discovered.'

A Learning from Experience exercise

Now try this for yourself. First, jot down six or seven recent, or not-so-recent, events that come to mind. Use a word or two to remind you of the experience. You can add to this list at any time. It becomes your index of experiences and the basis for you to show your competencies and strengths as well as your ability to learn how to improve things. Select one of those experiences and go through the Learning from Experience process. Imagine the kind of questions that Keith or Adam might ask as you go along and write a summary of your response as you complete each section.

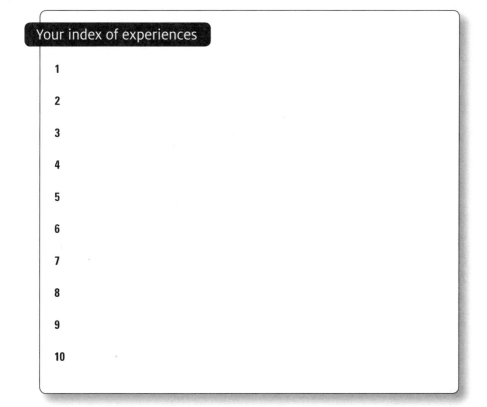

Your index of experiences

1

2

3

4

5

6

7

8

9

10

The story

Description of one experience.
Select a specific event or experience. Describe this experience to
a listener or Emotional Fitness coach if you have one.
Write down a summary of what you have said:

Discovery

What I have learned from that experience.
Next, read back what you have written in your story and explore, with
the help of your listener, what you now understand that you have learned
from the experience.
When you are ready, write down what you have learned (discovered about
yourself):

Proof

How I demonstrate that I use what I learned.

Discuss how you now use what you have learned from the experience just described. How can you demonstrate what you learned? Be creative and give examples to show what you know and can do and believe.

Write down your examples. These are (or will become) your strengths:

Ownership

What else I need to learn.

Talk with your listener about what else you need to learn in this area and summarize this for yourself.

Write down your summary:

Growth

What learning opportunities I plan to take up.

Finally, look at how you want to learn and what opportunities you want to carve out for yourself. Do you prefer to read things, practise them, go on courses, ask somebody, or what? Give yourself a realistic time for you to carry out your plan.

Write down your plan here:

At a later date (note the date now that you intend to do this), add notes to show that you have carried out your plan and the results you have achieved.

Now go back to one of the other experiences on your list and go through this process again. The more you try it for yourself, the more comfortable you will be trying it with someone else.

Treasure seeking
Tap the talent in your team at every meeting

Another bloody meeting

The sales meeting had been scheduled weeks ago, and now it was suddenly tomorrow. The five regional managers were to be there for the first day. The entire sales staff would come the following day, half of which would be spent meeting in their regional teams, and the remainder in what was intended to be a big motivational gathering. It was to be the first time that Marcus Baines would not preside over the meeting. The agenda that Adam printed out from his computer showed that it would be chaired by Evelyn Baines-Young.

He felt nervous as he left that evening, anticipating his performance with his own regional team for the first time, and deeply aware that he was going to lead the whole team in Evelyn's place in a few months' time. He had rehearsed what he wanted to do with his team and had all the statistics and targets. He had also received, as had the other regional sales managers, Evelyn's report and her outline for what she wanted from the meetings. The essence of it was to increase sales by nearly 20 per cent this year, an unprecedented target in a relatively stagnant or even shrinking market, especially with government and in the educational field.

The following morning's gloomy sky with its threat of rain did little to calm Adam's thoughts as he strode quickly through the park to the station as the first drops began to fall. He watched mournfully as the rain lashed at the windows of his train compartment, trying to concentrate on the day ahead. Something was unsettling him from the way that Evelyn had talked about the meeting and he couldn't quite work out what it was. He mentally shrugged his shoulders. Keith had told him that they would be looking at teams next time. Ah well, there would be a lot to learn from the next couple of days. What did he have to look for? The buried treasure. The train arrived and Adam stepped out into a clearing sky.

The morning was full of reports, statistics and forecasts, enlivened by a few demonstrations of new products to be launched in the coming weeks. Adam was welcomed into his first meeting as a regional sales manager. He wondered what the response was going to be when they discovered his leapfrogging to become their boss. They had accepted Evelyn well, but she had two things on her side. She was a member of the Baines family, and she was very straightforward and efficient in her job. They also had a grudging admiration for the way she had fired Patrick, one of their number and the one whom Adam had replaced. Adam felt he would be a bumbling mess in front of them. He smiled and accepted their congratulations, shaking hands firmly and looking each of his four colleagues in the eye. Good actor.

The afternoon was more of a brainstorming session, with all of them pitching in with their ideas and suggestions for increasing sales. Evelyn handled it brilliantly, thought Adam; taking note of all their ideas, distilling them into the best 10 by consensus and getting them recorded so that the regional managers could take them to their teams the next day.

He went home in a better frame of mind, although still unsettled. On the journey, he thought about the managers. What did he know about them? Where was the buried treasure? He realized that he knew very little about any of them apart from their sales records. Did he need to know more? Come to think of it, what did they know about him? He'd had the best sales figures for the past two years, so they were quite happy that he had been promoted. But if they knew about his next promotion and that he felt like a complete novice at management, they might not see him in too much of a positive light. He screwed up his eyes and shook his head quickly, trying to rid himself of these thoughts. As he opened his eyes, he instantly recalled his vision. He was here to help these people see the opportunities and go for them. He could get out of the way by not having concerns about how he seemed to others and by listening to them. He could hear their experiences and what they learned from them. And, once he had his next lesson from Keith, he would be able to work with them as a team.

The next morning Adam sat with his team of 11 sales representatives for the Midlands and Wales. He looked around at them. He knew them all; but he had little idea what they really brought to the table, what their aspirations were, or their worries and fears, or the treasure that Keith had assured him would be there in each of them. He shared the ideas that had come up from the managers' meeting the day before and asked them to consider how they could be put into practice. During the coffee and lunch breaks he managed to speak with each one of them. He noticed how Max always came across as positive and enthusiastic, encouraging others and obviously liked by them. Yes, he'd make a good manager with that team, Adam thought.

Nearly 50 people assembled into the office space that had been opened out for the occasion. Adam was only half surprised to see Marcus Baines there and wondered how Evelyn would handle it. It transpired that Marcus was there simply to start off the proceedings and introduce Evelyn as the daughter of 'the real founder of this company, Trevor Baines', as he put it. As the afternoon went on, Adam recognized the discomfort that he had been feeling. It was a highly energetic, award-giving event. Evelyn called up the best salespeople, congratulated everyone and told them how vital they were; and that they would have to sell a lot more over the next year.

The Group Dialogue

'The thing is,' said Adam, 'It was great; and yet there was something not quite right about it. I imagine that Evelyn's background and training from the cosmetics industry had something to do with it. Anyway, it didn't seem to fit with our situation.'

'What was it that didn't seem right?' asked Keith.

'Two things. First; it didn't feel very real. It was very upbeat and in a way entertaining, but I don't think it really reflected what people were feeling and thinking. They may have been very enthusiastic in the moment, but I wondered how long it would last. The other thing is that it was really good for those who received prizes for good sales results, but what does it do for the others? I suppose I felt it was a lost opportunity.'

'That's your cue, isn't it, Adam? How you can help to create opportunities for people; or rather help them to create opportunities. Today we're going to look at meetings, E-Fitness style. In this case you step into a different role; from that of coach or mentor to that of facilitator. It's just a case of applying your skills from working with an individual to working with a group. Now let's take a look at your sales team. What do you want to achieve in meeting with them?'

Adam thought for a moment. 'If you mean the team of sales reps, that might be different from when I'm running a meeting with the sales managers for the regions.'

'Well, pick one for now and tell me your goal.'

'Let's say my current team; and it would be helpful if I just think about the meeting I held with them last week. It was a bit out of my hands, because Evelyn had pretty well laid out what she expected and had discussed how she wanted the meetings run with all of the managers the day before. Essentially, my job was to motivate the reps by getting them involved in thinking about the ideas for growing sales. But at the end of the day, I don't think I had a very clear idea about many of them and what they really needed. Some were really engaged; others were quiet. The best bit was during the breaks when I managed to have a brief chat with each of them.'

'Good,' said Keith. 'If you had your way, and you were meeting them next week, what would be different?'

'I keep remembering what you said about finding that buried treasure. What I'd like to do is to discover the talent that lies in the team and to bring out the best in everyone. Some perform well and they could help to inspire the others. But I've no idea what makes them tick and somehow I would like to find out.'

'What else?'

'Well, of course, I want them to increase their sales. I'd like all of them to be more successful. I'd like less complaining and more positive ideas and input. I'd like the ones who feel less confident to get that confidence and the ones who come across as too high pressure to tone down a bit. I want to instil a greater sense of loyalty to the company and a much better grasp of the products and the operating processes, so that they can talk with greater knowledge to the customers. Actually, I think that most of them could do with better sales skills, which means they have to connect with the customer and listen to them better. Oh, and they need to have really good self-discipline and stick to the systems for getting and following up leads and maintaining their records of client calls.'

'There's quite an agenda for starters, Adam. And what do you think they may want from the meetings?'

'That's a good question. I don't really know. I do know what I wanted as a sales rep. More accurately, I knew what I didn't want; like information that I could have got by e-mail, or a list of things that had gone wrong, or exhortations to do better. Patrick obviously had no idea how to run a meeting. He always seemed quite uncomfortable and I certainly want to come across as knowing what I'm doing. And I don't want to hog the meeting either and make it look as though I want to control everything. I remember ...' Adam stopped; looked at Keith through lowered eyelids.

'That's okay,' said Keith. 'You probably remember when I used to run our meetings and talked most of the time. I've learned a lot since then. In the E-Fitness meeting, which we call a Group Dialogue, the team leader, or facilitator, has a set of goals. You can pick any or all of them. The facilitator wants to see enhanced communication and listening, a greater understanding of the topics discussed, decisions taken that reflect real concerns, people using their emotional intelligence as well as their intellectual abilities, and individuals taking greater responsibility for their own actions. The results are that problems are solved in more creative and long-lasting ways, people feel equally supported and challenged, the follow-up encourages desired changes to take place, and overall team performance is enhanced.'

'You might have to repeat that, Keith. I couldn't quite take it all in.'

'Don't worry; it's written down and we can go through it later. More to the point is that the structure for these Group Dialogue meetings can deal with those goals and also the objectives that you defined earlier. Such as getting to know people's talents, increasing their sales success, engendering greater loyalty and so on. It also ensures that the things you don't want don't happen. Nobody will hog the meeting or reel off a list of information. And decisions will always be made. What's more, the meeting is exactly in line with your overall purpose of providing opportunities for people to learn and improve.

'Now, unlike our other sessions, we can't practise a Group Dialogue here; so I will go through the structure and you can practise it back at work. It doesn't matter what team, or group of people, you work with. We'll talk about that later. This system works equally well with an executive team or an operational team or group of administrative staff. And when we combine it with Learning from Experience, it's even more powerful in how it can bring positive results.'

Keith brought out his binder and laid it on the table, moving the empty coffee cups to one side. Adam bent his head over the page as Keith turned it around for him to see.

Group dialogue

The seven-stage structure:

1   Presentation. Draw up an agenda from the team and invite one person to present their topic.

2   Clarification. Invite the others to ask questions.

3   Summaries. Everyone writes down the essence of what they have understood.

4   Presenter's summary. The speaker gives their own summary.

5   Action. Everyone else writes down the action they would take.

6   Presenter's action. The speaker says what they themselves will do.

7   Implications. The meaning and action for everyone arising from this.

'As you see,' said Keith, 'there are seven stages in the structure for this meeting. Trust me, it's not like any meeting you are likely to have been part of. In a way, we are using and adapting Power Listening within a group setting, so we have to set up a contract to start with. The contract you will have with your team consists of two things: the procedure for the meeting, which will be spelled out to them so that they understand what will be taking place, and the agenda, which you will formulate from the group. This all happens before the first stage and the actual meeting gets underway.'

'You mean,' asked Adam, his eyebrows arching, 'that I don't go in with a prepared agenda? That's against everything I was ever taught about meetings.'

'That's right,' said Keith. 'If you remember from that first famous and brilliant training video, *Meetings Bloody Meetings* by John Cleese, we learned that one of the main failings of most meetings was not having a clear agenda. However, the purpose of this meeting is a little different; plus we have a very specific structure that allows the leader of the meeting to maintain the order that John Cleese's character fell down on.

'As the facilitator, you will first of all go briefly through this structure, saying that the meeting is going to have a different format. Then, a little like the brainstorming session you had the other day, you are going to ask people what they want on the agenda. This is also a little different, in a very important way. Instead of asking what items they want to discuss, you ask each person to think about one thing that is significant to them at the present time in relation to their work. For example, Adam, how would you answer that question?'

'Well, what's uppermost in my mind at this point is how I am going to tackle my new job when I've hardly got into the current one. But I'm not sure I want to discuss that with my team.'

'Where would you be prepared to talk about it, and in what circumstances?'

Adam hesitated. 'If anywhere, maybe I'd talk about it with Evelyn and Sam; but that's not really a group, is it?'

'Not quite big enough for a Group Dialogue. You'd need at least one other person.'

'I suppose the obvious ones are Marcus Baines and Stella Oxberry. Stella's the admin and HR director, as you know. I don't know her very well, but I have a feeling she'd be good at this. The one time I had an interview with her, she listened really well. Oh, and you asked about the circumstances. I don't know if the directors meet now on a regular basis; or if so what they discuss. When I'm a director I'd like to think that we will meet to review what's going on and plan ahead.'

'Then that becomes your natural team for you to discuss those kinds of things with. We'll come to that later. For the time being, let's concentrate on your own sales team. You go round to each member of the team, asking for one significant thing that is going on in their work and you write it up on a whiteboard. You may get some of the same things; you might get items that are seen as problems, ideas, even complaints. List them all up, marking the name or initial of the person saying it. You have 11 in your team, so it's just the right size – actually, about the largest you can do this with without splitting into two groups.

'Now you have your agenda of items. You are probably only going to discuss one or two at most this time, supposing that you have an hour or less for your meeting, so your next task is to select which one to start with. Ask the group to suggest one. Sometimes it's obvious; sometimes it may take a little negotiation to select one. Once you have the item, you will invite the person who suggested it to present it. Before that, you will go through the rules and explain the purpose and the structure to them. For the purpose, you can select all or any of those that I suggested earlier, or whatever fits your own situation.' Keith turned back the page of his folder for Adam to see. 'Here are those benefits I mentioned before. You can define your own purpose from that, depending upon what you want to achieve from the Group Dialogue.'

Benefits of the Group Dialogue include:

- enhanced communication and listening skills in a group;

- greater understanding of issues;

- decisions taken reflect real concerns;

- people use their emotional intelligence as well as their intellectual abilities;

- individuals take greater responsibility for their own actions;

- problems are solved in a more creative and long-lasting way;

- people feel equally supported and challenged;

- follow-up encourages desired changes to take place;

- team performance is enhanced.

The set-up

On the way in to work, Adam mused over how he could carry out the action he had agreed with Keith. He had to find a group to practise on. He didn't feel ready to ask Evelyn to try it out on the group of directors. After all, he wasn't one yet. And he had just met with his sales team and couldn't justify bringing them all in again so soon. There was the team of regional sales managers; but he was still one of them and he wasn't going to jeopardize the delicate situation by setting himself up as a facilitator without giving away the fact that something was in the air and he would soon be their boss.

He still hadn't resolved his dilemma as he walked up the concrete steps to the front door of Baines Electronics. He hardly noticed who the two figures were that were standing chatting at the top of the steps, until he reached them. Marcus Baines and Matthew, the maintenance man, were chatting and laughing as if they were old friends. When Adam reached them, Matthew, the echo of a laugh still in his voice, said, 'I've got work to go to; can't stand around gossiping like this,' and went off chuckling to himself.

'Good morning, Adam,' chortled the boss. 'You know, I always like passing the time of day with Matthew. He's been around for years. Knows everyone and everything that goes on. Wonderful source of information, that man. Straight as they come; and he can do anything with a hammer and a screwdriver in his hand. Come to think of it, I don't think I've ever seen him without a tool in his hand.'

By the time he reached his office, Adam had formulated a plan.

Practice session

Eight heads turned to look at him – with some suspicion, Adam thought. He reminded himself of the mantra. Relax and concentrate. Stella, the admin and HR director, had given her blessing; as had Evelyn. Now he was in the boardroom with Andrea, Marcus Baines's PA, and the seven people who reported directly to her. He knew a couple of them. They consisted of two admin assistants, the personnel assistant, two wages clerks, Claudia the receptionist, and Matthew.

Andrea introduced Adam and passed the meeting over to him.

'I really want to thank you all for being here,' began Adam. 'You are probably wondering what this is about and I'm going to be absolutely up front about it. I'm taking some training from someone who is coaching me in some management techniques that I have found to be really helpful and positive. I think they will help us at Baines Electronics and I would really like your comments at the end on whether you find this useful. I wanted a group to, well, kind of practise on and one that I didn't already have any connection with.'

There were a few nudges and head turnings. Adam cleared his throat.

'I know you are all busy, and I can promise you that we won't go a minute over the hour we have set aside. Basically, we are going to have a meeting; but it will be a different kind of meeting from the usual. My purpose here is for you, this admin and support services team, to have a chance to decide on some things that could make your work run more easily and efficiently for you and to look at some ideas you may have to improve things. How does that sound?'

A couple of nods went around the table. Andrea said, 'We're always looking for improvements; so anything that helps will be good.' Matthew shifted in his chair, giving out a metallic clank.

'For this to work,' Adam persisted, 'all of you will have to take part. I'll really need your help with that. To make it easier, I want to give out a few ground rules, which anyone can add to. First of all, unless we all agree otherwise, nothing anyone says here will go outside the room. Is that agreed?'

More heads nodded this time, and more vigorously.

'Second, there is a very clear structure to this meeting and I will take you through it as we go along. We will set up our agenda, then we will select what to focus on, and the person who brought up the topic will say a bit more about it. The others will listen and ask questions that help us to understand more about it. By the end, we will have reached a decision or found a solution that will help us all. I will take you through all the stages as we go along. Do you have any questions or anything you want to add at this point?'

Silence. A little shuffling. A hand went up. 'Yes, Riva.' Adam reminded himself to thank Andrea for putting name cards in front of each person.

'You said that everything will be confidential, right?'

'Yes, absolutely.'

'So what if we do come up with something? How will we make sure anything happens?'

'Good question, Riva. First of all, what will always remain confidential are the details of who says what and how anyone might feel about things. However, if you remember, I said that if we all agree that something should be taken forward outside here, then we will do that.'

Nobody else had anything to add, so Adam continued.

'Now we are going to see what kind of things you might want to improve or change. Anything that seems to bother you or that you are having problems with at work; or perhaps something that you have noticed or been thinking about that could make a difference. I'll give you a moment to think about the one thing that you think would make your working life easier or could improve how we do things around here.'

Adam looked around at the seven faces looking expectantly, blankly or puzzled back at him. He had to add something.

'Let me just say that anything goes here. Don't forget that this is for me to learn as much as it is to help the company and this team. And nobody can be wrong.'

'All right, then.' It was Matthew. 'I have to say that I don't really fit in here; on the other hand I don't fit in anywhere else. Or I suppose you could say I have to fit in everywhere. Anyway, this is my little beef, if you want to call it that. I don't know if it's what you're looking for, but I might as well start it off for you.'

'Thank you, Matthew. Whatever you want to say will fit in perfectly.'

Matthew's expression didn't quite show belief in that statement. It didn't stop him. 'Well, anyway, it's like this. I get this list of jobs to do every day. All the time really. Some are big jobs, most are little things. Usually they come through Andrea, but sometimes one of the supervisors will catch me and ask for something to be fixed. It turns out that everything is always urgent and I try to get everything done within a reasonable time. I have to decide which things really are urgent. I mean, if there's a repair needed to keep production going, I'm going to do that before fixing a hinge on an office door, aren't I? What I want to know is; who should decide which things should happen first?'

Adam stood up, went over to the whiteboard on the wall, speaking as he wrote. 'That's a great start, Matthew, thank you. You seem to have said that you have a question about priorities and who should decide them; is that right?'

'Exactly. Yes – that's just it.'

Adam wrote up 'Who should decide on priorities?' and wrote beside it 'Matthew'.

'Let's go around the room. Jenny, what do you have for us this morning?'

Jenny, one of the wages clerks, talked about the constantly changing government requirements and how she was always trying to keep up with the tables and keep on top of her regular duties. Adam wrote it up.

He wrote up the other five items, too. Finally, this is what was on the whiteboard:

Who should decide on priorities?: Matthew

Dealing with required changes: Jenny

Having a place to put visitors: Claudia

Having an adequate interview room: Maria

Catching up with the new filing system: Riva

Not enough time – too much work: Sharon

Balancing everything: Andrea

'This is our current list of things to attend to,' said Adam, surveying his handiwork. 'We are probably only going to get through one, or maybe two with the time we have, so either we can do this again, if you find it useful, or you can deal with them in your own way. Our next thing is to decide which of these seven topics to talk about. Any suggestions?'

It was quickly unanimous. Adam wasn't sure whether it was because it was the first, or because it was safer for the others to pick Matthew, or because it was a subject that they could all relate to. He didn't think it mattered. Keith had told him there was treasure to be found everywhere.

'Well now, Matthew; it looks like you have the opportunity to talk more about your topic of priorities. Before you do that, I just want to go over those ground rules in more detail. I will ask Matthew to tell us more about his situation regarding the maintenance work requests he gets and how to put them in priority order. After that, the floor is open to the rest of you to ask him any questions that will help you to understand fully what he says. Often, the problem with communication is that we assume we understand, but we don't really. On the other hand we think we are supposed to know and don't want to feel foolish by asking questions, when all the time nobody else quite gets it either. This meeting actually invites you to ask any question you like, to help us all to understand something better. So again, no questions are off bounds as long as the intention is to make something clearer. When we have finished asking questions, I am going to ask each one of you to write down a brief summary of what you have heard and understood.'

Adam waited while he looked around the room. He saw eyes widen and one or two heads go down.

'Look,' he said, 'this is new to all of us, so try not to worry about getting anything wrong. You can't be wrong; that's the beauty of this; and we are all going to learn something. Especially me.'

Adam handed the sheets of paper around, noticing his hands trembling a little. Fear or excitement? Andrea had already supplied everyone with the ubiquitous Baines Electronics pen. Everyone looked down at the page in front of them.

Presentation

'Right then, Matthew,' said Adam brightly, not feeling bright at all. 'Tell us more about the maintenance requests.'

'Not much more to say, really,' said Matthew. Adam felt his stomach curdle.

'Well, remind us what you've said.' He had a fleeting image of Keith smiling at him.

'The thing is, I'm not really sure if I always get things done in the right order. It makes sense to me, but who's to say? See, the other day I had Tom, the supervisor in the audio division pleading with me to fix a workstation that had developed a wobble. It wasn't much, but his operative couldn't use the table like that. It would take me about 30 minutes to fix it. The trouble was I had a list as long as your arm

of things that needed doing and half of them were marked "urgent".'
He looked over at Andrea. 'Am I supposed to go to Andrea every time
to ask if I should do things, or take my own initiative?'

Matthew sat back. His face was flushed. He wiped his forehead
with the back of his hand.

Clarification

Andrea spoke first. 'I don't know why you'd even ask that, Matthew;
I thought we had discussed it a long time ago.'

Adam jumped in just as he saw Matthew about to respond.

'Okay, let's hold it there. Thank you for that, Matthew. Remember
that this isn't a usual kind of meeting. Our next stage is to ask
Matthew questions that help us to clarify things so that we understand what is going on. I'm going to ask you to reframe what you
have said to Matthew, Andrea, and ask him a question. Our job here
is to listen to him and understand what he's saying. That means we
must do our best to keep ourselves out of the way.'

Andrea shot him a glance that felt like a dagger to Adam.
'Relax,' he said to himself. 'Concentrate,' he thought, completing the
mantra.

'Very well; I'll try,' said Andrea. 'Matthew, why did you ask if you
can use your initiative?' She bit her lip, as though holding back the
rest of what she wanted to say.

'Ah, well,' drawled Matthew, 'You might remember about six
months ago there was this big to-do over a backlog of maintenance
work, with people complaining that I was giving preference to some
over others. Your boss, Mrs Oxberry, sent this memo around saying
everything was to go through you. Of course, it doesn't always
happen, as I say, and then I get complaints anyway.'

Adam saw Andrea about to speak and gently opened his hand
towards her. 'Thanks, Matthew and Andrea. I want to go around the
table. Who else has a question for Matthew?'

Claudia cleared her throat. 'I'd like to ask Matthew something.
How does the order of work get decided now?'

Matthew answered. The questions began to flow more easily. A
picture emerged. When everyone had asked a question, Adam asked
if there were any more before he asked them to make a summary of

what they had heard. Riva had a secondary question. There were no more.

Summaries

'Great,' chirped Adam. 'Next, I want each of you, except for Matthew at this point, to write down a brief summary of what you have heard and understood. Read what the instructions say. You are asked to write down the essence; in other words, get to the core meaning of Matthew's message. You are not expected to remember and write down the details of everything. Also, please put yourself in the place of Matthew as much as you can. It might be a stretch to imagine yourself as the maintenance man; or in your cases woman, but please give it a try. It really helps you to understand it when you write it down from Matthew's perspective, which is why you start by writing, 'As Matthew, I ...', rather than saying 'Matthew said that he ...' and so on.'

As they bent forward to pick up their pens, he caught Andrea's eye. He mouthed 'Thank you' to her and nodded. Her features softened. Matthew looked at his watch. Twenty-five minutes left.

They spent what seemed an eternity writing down. It was probably only a couple of minutes. When the last of them finished, Adam asked each to read out what she had written, without adding anything to it.

Andrea started. 'I heard Matthew say "I am confused about how the decisions are taken to plan the maintenance work requests. I feel that my own judgement is not respected and that I am not backed up when I do take a decision."'

Adam watched Matthew's jaw slacken. 'Thank you, Andrea. Who's next?'

Claudia volunteered. 'I heard Matthew say "I have a lot of experience and skill and it isn't always acknowledged. I would like to handle the job requests in my own way, with a second opinion if there is a dispute."'

Maria was next. 'This all sounds pretty similar. I heard Matthew say "I want to be free to use my initiative. I understand the importance of keeping the production moving and will always give that precedence. I want to feel that I have the backing of management when I take decisions."'

By the time all six had given their summaries there was a distinct change of atmosphere in the room. What had been a tension in the air now felt like a relaxed sense of accomplishment. Adam knew that what he felt now was a rising excitement.

Presenter's summary

'Now, Matthew; you have heard what everyone has said. I would like you to write down your own summary in your own words. While Matthew is doing that, the rest of you can take a couple of minutes' break.'

Matthew sat poring over the piece of paper, holding his pen awkwardly, clearly preferring the screwdriver in his hand. The women went over to the coffee machine, chatting quietly among themselves. Adam stayed in his chair, willing the clock to be obedient and not go too fast.

A few minutes later, Matthew read his own statement. 'I felt that my experience has not been respected. I kept quiet when I should have said something. The result was that my initiative was taken away from me and I have been left in the middle, trying to keep everyone happy. I would like to take decisions and to have the backing from management.'

The effort of saying this seemed colossal as Matthew slumped back in his chair. The silence was as thick as treacle. Adam broke it. 'Thank you, Matthew. Now I want everyone else to write down what action you will take, imagining again that you are Matthew. Write it down in the space you have. Matthew, you can take a short break now.'

Action

This time, Riva volunteered to start. 'As Matthew,' she began, 'I will look at my current list of jobs and make my own order of precedence, which I will take to Andrea and discuss it with her. I realize that I may not have all the necessary information and Andrea may help to fill that in for me. I will then negotiate how I could make these decisions myself and ask Andrea or perhaps Stella how I can have their support and second opinions when there is a dispute.'

Riva was not the only one to come up with such actions. Others were similar, with suggestions to speak out when he felt not respected, to have a regular meeting with Andrea, to chat to any of the members of the team when he felt the need to get something off his chest and to post a notice, prominently displayed, of the current state of maintenance jobs and their progress.

Matthew had been busy scribbling notes while the others were talking, even asking once or twice for someone to repeat what she had just said.

Presenter's action

'One more thing for each of you to write down,' said Adam. 'Matthew, you can write down your own action. The rest of you, please answer the last question on your sheet. What are the personal and professional implications for you of what Matthew has shared and from this process?'

When Matthew read out his action statement, his voice sounded stronger, more determined than before. 'I am going to discuss this more with Andrea first and then Stella Oxberry. I will suggest that I am the one to get all the maintenance requests and make up the work order. If there is any doubt or dispute I will take it to Andrea or Mrs Oxberry. I will make a copy of the work order and stick it on the noticeboard every day.' He looked around the room. 'It's time,' he said, 'that I enjoyed my work again.'

It was as though a plume of steam gushed out of a cauldron as everyone let out a breath at the same time.

Implications

'Thank you, Matthew. Now I'm going to ask each of you to read what you have just written.'

'I'll start.' It was Andrea. 'This has been an eye-opener for me. I am going to do whatever I can to support Matthew and to give him a free hand to take the initiative in deciding the work order. As far as I'm concerned, this has been an extra piece of work that I can do without. I took it on because I thought that Matthew didn't want to do it. Now I know I got it all wrong. This means that I have to improve how I communicate.'

Sharon, one of the two admin assistants, went next. 'I said there was not enough time and too much work. Hearing this, I am going to prioritize my work more. I know that Riva is really good at that and I am going to ask her to help me. In exchange I will help her with the filing system.'

Everyone had a statement. Everyone had something significant to do or to change. Fifty-five minutes had elapsed since the start of their meeting.

'Finally,' said Adam, 'I would like your comments and feedback about this meeting.'

Maria, the personnel assistant, burst out with it. 'That was amazing. It's the first time I have sat in a meeting and felt really engaged in it all the time, even though I might not have said much. At first I wondered why I was here; and then when Matthew started I thought it had nothing to do with me. But as it went on, I found myself thinking how he could do something about his situation and I also began to think I could do something about my own. In this last piece I came up with an idea for how we could have a better space for interviewing people and what I can do about it. It's amazing,' she repeated.

Even where others were more muted, it was clear to Adam that this had been a success greater than his imagination dared take him. That thought was reinforced when Andrea made the suggestion just as they were about to end.

'Why don't we do this again? Perhaps it could become a regular meeting; say once a month. Would you be prepared to run it for us, Adam?'

He couldn't wait to get back to his office to fire off a text message to Keith. 'Found some treasure!' it said.

Group Dialogue

Date: ....

Presenter: ....

Summary

Write down your own summary of what you have heard from the presenter. You are seeking to find the essence of what has been shared, including what you have noticed as well as the words you have heard. Start your summary with 'I heard (presenter's name) say ...'.

Action

Having listened carefully to the presenter's own summary (not your own!) write down the action steps you would take as though you were the presenter. Start your action points with 'As (presenter's name), I will ...'.

Implications

What are the personal/professional implications for you of what the presenter has shared and from this process?

E-Fitness action learning

'You are ready to take a step up,' said Keith. 'Find a way to run a Group Dialogue with your senior management team. Only this time, incorporate Learning from Experience. You will find that this might be the best way to introduce E-Fitness into the organization. The only difference is that, instead of leaving the agenda open, you define it a bit more narrowly and your questions afterwards will be slightly different. A man called Reginald Revans developed a process called Action Learning more than 60 years ago and it's similar to that. Here's an example of how we use it in E-Fitness coaching; but you can play with the words so that they are perfectly relevant.' Keith slipped out his folder, laid the sheet on the table.

'This will really enable you to draw out the talent in people. I guarantee you that when you have finished, two things will happen. Everyone will come away with something of value for themselves, and since you are going to be doing this with the decision makers, they will want it spread through the company.'

'When am I going to find the time to do my own work?' asked Adam.

Keith put his head to one side. Adam was familiar with the look.

E-Fitness Action Learning

The seven-stage adapted structure:

1   The story. Draw up a list of recent work experiences or observations from the team and invite one person to present their story.

2   Discovery. Invite the others to ask questions for clarification, focusing on what was learned from the presenter's story.

3   Proof. Everyone (except the presenter) writes down the essence of what they have understood and reads it back.

4   Ownership. The presenter writes and reads back their own summary, including what they themselves need to learn.

5   Growth. Everyone else writes down the action they would take as the presenter and reads this back.

6   Growth. The presenter writes down and says what they themselves will do.

7   Implications. The meaning, action and follow-up for individuals, the team and the organization arising from what has been learned and decided.

E-Fitness Action Learning

Date: ....

Presenter: ....

Summary

Write down your own summary of what you have heard from the presenter. You are seeking to find the essence of what has been shared, including what you have noticed as well as the words you have heard. Start your summary with 'I heard (presenter's name) say ...'.

Action

Having listened carefully to the presenter's own summary (not your own!) write down the action steps you would take as though you were the presenter. Start your action points with 'As (presenter's name), I will ...'.

Implications

What are the implications and actions for you, for the team and for the organization of what you have learned from the E-Fitness Action Learning session?

Exercise

While Adam plans his next move, try it out for yourself. Consider the following:

- Take a look at a team. What do you know about the talent that exists? How much of it do you see?

- Describe the role of the E-Fitness facilitator.

- Decide upon the team or group that you will test this out with.

- How will you approach them?

- What is your purpose in running a Group Dialogue or E-Fitness Action Learning session?

- How will you define success?

- When will you run the meeting?

- What follow-up do you want?

- How will you deal with the feedback?

- What support do you want?

The energy equation

05

Using the Workscale to transform negative into positive

The energy impact

Sam was in one of his moods. The three of them, Evelyn, Sam and Adam, sat in Evelyn's office. They hadn't met for a couple of weeks. Word of the success of the meeting that Adam had held with the admin and support team had reached Evelyn within a day. Marcus had told her after Andrea had told Marcus how helpful it had been. Evelyn spoke with Stella who had confirmed that her staff had raved over it, and then called Adam to suggest that they get together again with Sam. She didn't want to lose the momentum.

It looked as though the momentum, as far as Sam was concerned, was already lost. 'How long is this going to take?' he enquired brusquely. 'I've got a crisis going on with one of the sections – one of my supervisors is off sick and the designer is driving me nuts.'

It flitted though Adam's mind that he'd love to do a Group Dialogue with Sam right now, but didn't have a group to do it in. How would Keith handle this?

Evelyn was already handling it in her own way. 'Tell you what, Sam; if you really have to get back to the shop floor, please do so. But it's exactly those situations you are facing that we need to discuss and see how we can handle in better ways. What have you learned from the management book you are reading?'

Sam glared at her. 'Reading stuff is one thing. Handling it on the ground is another. Anyway, I haven't got past the first chapter yet.'

'What is the book, anyway?' asked Evelyn.

Sam's answer came back briefly and gruffly. 'It's *The Art of War*, if you must know. By Sun Tzu.'

Adam watched Evelyn's eyebrows raise and felt his own mirror them.

'That's a difficult book, Sam. A tough one to start with.' Evelyn hesitated. 'Congratulations for going with it; there are a lot of wise pointers for how to lead in business as well as warfare. You are obviously anxious to get back, so I suggest that we set a time that will work for everyone. I have spoken with Stella Oxberry and with Marcus and they would like to join us.' She didn't look at Adam; concentrated on Sam.

'Whatever you want.' Sam rose slowly, almost reluctantly, turned stiffly and shuffled towards the door. He turned to them as he reached it. 'I'll get on, then. See you later. Just let me know when you want to meet. Right after lunch is usually best for me; the mornings are just too hectic, and the end of the day there's always something that comes up.' He closed the door behind him.

'Phew,' uttered Evelyn as she faced Adam. 'I'm not used to dealing with someone like Sam. Can't quite make him out. I'm not unhappy that he went; it gives me a chance to consider how to move forward. I want to know more about what you are learning with this coach of yours.'

'As a matter of fact he used to work here. He was a sales rep and then a regional sales manager, my boss actually, before you came here. His name is Keith Parkinson. After he left, he trained as an Emotional Fitness coach. He's been using some of the techniques with me and teaching them to me. I have to say, it's made a big difference to me already. I still have a whole lot to learn, but I am getting to be a much better listener than I was, and that meeting I tried the other day – well, I meant to tell you about it but there hasn't been much time.'

'Oh, I've heard about that, Adam, and not just from people who were there. It's got around. It's what I want to talk to you about. I discussed it with Marcus and Stella, and they would both like to see what it's about. That's why I invited them to join you and me and Sam. It also meant that Stella had to know about the changes; so Marcus told her. Now all of us directors know, or director-in-waiting in your case, and have pledged to keep it to ourselves. So my question is, will you do that group thing with us?'

Adam recalled the butterfly. Its wings were already causing a breeze. 'If that's what you'd like, I'd love to.' He couldn't have worked it better however he might have planned it.

'Great. I'll set it up,' said Evelyn. 'Meanwhile, what do we do about Sam? He seems to be so moody. One moment he's positive and enthusiastic, the next he's down in the dumps, irritable and difficult to communicate with. Why don't you ask your coach? Maybe he has some ideas. What are we paying him for this? And I assume he keeps anything you say to himself.'

'I'll certainly ask Keith. Actually he's not charging – it's part of the practice that he has to do to complete his certificate. We must certainly pay him after this. And yes, of course it's totally confidential. He showed me the ethical agreement he signed for his professional association.'

* * * * * *

'Ah yes – Sam,' mused Keith. 'I'm not sure whether it's an advantage or disadvantage that I know him. He is certainly an example of someone whose emotional energy fluctuates and affects others around him. Perhaps, rather than talk about Sam, we can look at how to discover and handle the positive and negative emotional energies that people bring to work.'

'You're right about energy,' said Adam. 'I actually feel my own energy drop when Sam is like that. I wonder what his workers feel like when he's miserable.'

'You've put your finger on the problem, Adam. The kind of emotional energy transmitted by people, especially when they are in authority, tends to be catching. Remember you talked about Marcus Baines's inspiration? You seemed to be caught up by that and wanting your own. Now you say that Sam's negative energy brings you down. That makes it vital that we provide support to those in key positions to maintain and, where needed, bring up their levels of emotional fitness.'

'By listening to them, you mean?'

'That, certainly; but in E-Fitness coaching we have a tool that helps people to measure their own levels of positive and negative emotional energy. Eugene Heimler, back in the seventies, called this the levels of people's satisfactions and frustrations. He developed a scale called the scale of Human Social Functioning. In E-Fitness, we have a much simpler scale designed for the work environment. It's called the Workscale. That's what I am going to show you today.'

The Workscale

Keith brought out his folder and took out a sheaf of paper. 'Take a look at this,' he said. 'As always, the best way to learn something is to try it out.'

Adam spent a few minutes looking at the questions and giving a value for each of them. Some were harder than others; he found he had to think about several to make sense of the questions for himself. Keith had told him to give as broad a definition to the key words as he liked. Even as he filled in the numbers, he knew how different some of them would have been before he started seeing Keith. When he had finished, he added up each column. The scores came to 66 and 41.

'What does that mean?' asked Adam.

Keith gave one of his enigmatic smiles. 'That's really what I get to ask you. The 66 indicates the total of satisfactions, or positive emotional energy. The 41 is your frustration total, or your negative emotional energy. I want you to note that positive and negative don't mean good and bad; they are both important. Without negative energy, where is the motivation? It is often the main source of our creativity. The problem is when you have more negative than positive, it tends to drag you down. So all I can really see from your Workscale is that you have about two-thirds more satisfaction than frustration, which seems to show that you are functioning pretty well and have a fairly healthy level of E-Fitness. What the scores actually mean is for you to say. The Workscale is different from almost any other kind of test, in that it is the person who completes the scores who defines their meanings, not the person who administers it, or the originator of the tool. Remember, E-Fitness is about empowerment and all the tools reflect this.'

WORKSCALE

Before we start, give a value from 0 to 20 to each of the following 10 questions. For example, if you feel you have a great deal of pleasure from work, give a high score; if you don't feel poverty at all, give a low score; if you feel about halfway on a pressure scale, give about 10 for how much pressure you feel. If you are unsure what a question means, decide on the meaning that makes sense to you.

NAME_____ DATE_____

Score each question on a scale 0–20.

1 How much PLEASURE do I get from my work?........................... ☐

2 How much PAIN do I have at work?................................... ☐

3 How much PURPOSE do I have in my work?............................ ☐

4 How much do PROBLEMS weigh me down? .... ☐

5 How much do I feel I'm in the right PLACE? .... ☐

6 How much PREJUDICE do I feel against me? .... ☐

7 How much POWER do I feel I have? .... ☐

8 How much POVERTY do I feel I have? .... ☐

9 How much PEACE of mind do I feel? .... ☐

10 How much PRESSURE do I feel is on me? .... ☐

Total scores (two columns) .... ☐ ☐

'That's refreshing,' murmured Adam. 'Usually, after I've filled these things out, someone tells me who I am. Not that they are wrong. It's just that they always seem to put me into a box, some kind of psychological framework, which doesn't feel that helpful.'

'That's part of the reason I found E-Fitness to be so valuable. And let's face it, coaches aren't psychologists and have no business applying psychological testing instruments. It's not my job to analyse what you are saying. It's my job to help you to make sense of your own words, actions and feelings, and then to help you find and take the decisions that will enhance your work and your life. The Workscale is one of the tools that does that.'

Keith turned the page of the document in front of Adam. 'Now I want you to go through each of the questions again. This time, after you have transferred the number you wrote earlier, I'd like you to tell me what your own score means to you. I will use Power Listening. When you are ready, you will write down your own summary of the meaning. We'll start with the first two – which are denoted by the key words "pleasure" and "pain" – so that you get the hang of it. It's very valuable to go through this with a coach first. After that it's a very useful tool that can be used by anyone. We'll talk about ways you can use it at work later.'

How much PLEASURE do I get from my work?

Give a score for that question, on a scale from 0 to 20. The more pleasure you feel you have, the higher the score; the less you feel, the lower the score.

Put your score in this box:

What does my score for PLEASURE mean to me?

How much PAIN do I have at work?

Again, give a score for this anywhere between 0 and 20. Lots of pain will get a high score; little pain will get a low score.

What does my score for PAIN mean to me?

Adam wrote down the values he had entered before. He put 15 for 'How much pleasure do I get from my work?', and 6 for 'How much pain do I have at work?'

'Now tell me what that 15 out of 20 for pleasure means to you,' asked Keith.

'It was just a general feeling at first. Actually, I do enjoy my work a lot, but there are some things that I find get me down. I get pleasure from the people I work with. I used to love it when I got a good order, but that's changing now that I'm the manager. I had great connections with most of my customers. I do enjoy the other sales teams and I'm beginning to like working with Evelyn. I think what gives me most pleasure is in knowing that I make a difference to the business.'

'What kind of difference?' Keith enquired.

'I always think that when we get an order, the people at Baines will still have work; and the products we make are useful to people in their lives.'

'Anything else make up that 15?'

'I'm getting excited about the possibilities for me to have a greater role. I am beginning to look forward to this whole idea of inspiring others to see the possibilities, and I'm going to have the perfect opportunity to do that in my new job.'

'What would the other 5 consist of, if you had scored 20?'

'I wouldn't have this feeling of it being too much for me to handle. It's that question of "What if I fail?" hanging over my head.'

'Now I'd like you to make a summary and write down what you've said about what gives you pleasure from your work and what doesn't.'

Adam wrote down his summary in the space; then he read it back to Keith.

'My score for pleasure means that I enjoy making a difference in my work, and I see the bigger picture. I enjoy the challenge of inspiring others. I like the people I work with. It's 15, not 20, because I still feel nervous that I might fail in my job as sales director.'

'Thank you, Adam. Now take a look at what you gave for the next question and tell me what it means to you.'

They went through the same process, Keith asking questions, Adam clarifying what he meant and summarizing it on the page. They did this for all of the 10 questions. Keith asked Adam to look at what he had written.

How much PLEASURE do I get from my work?

Give a score for that question, on a scale from 0 to 20. The more pleasure you feel you have, the higher the score; the less you feel, the lower the score.

Put your score in this box.

What does my score for PLEASURE mean to me?

'My score for pleasure means that I enjoy making a difference in my work, and I see the bigger picture. I enjoy the challenge of inspiring others. I like the people I work with. It's 15, not 20, because I still feel nervous that I might fail in my job as sales director.'

How much PAIN do I have at work?

Again, give a score for this anywhere between 0 and 20. Lots of pain will get a high score; little pain will get a low score.

What does my score for PAIN mean to me?

'Nothing much physical. It's mostly to do with the fear of failure, plus the actual amount of work I'm having to do is wearing and I sometimes get headaches.'

How much PURPOSE do I have in my work?

A great deal of purpose will give you a score towards the 20 mark, very little purpose will have you hovering nearer the 0 point. If you are not sure, or you waver between feeling lots of purpose and not much, you'll probably give a score around the 10 region. Since it's how you feel right now, it has to be right.

What does my score for PURPOSE mean to me?

'This must have gone up a lot since we've been meeting and I decided to take the promotion. I now feel that I have a mission and I am clear about it. It's much more than hitting sales targets; it's about helping people to see the possibilities and be successful. Maybe it will be 20 when I see that I am doing that.'

How much do PROBLEMS weigh me down?

A lot? Give a high score. Not much? Give a low one on the 0 to 20 scale. Notice that the question isn't about how many problems you have or haven't got; it's about how much you feel they affect you personally and weigh you down.

What does my score for PROBLEMS mean to me?

'I see these as challenges. Sometimes I do feel a bit overwhelmed with all there is to do and learn. And dealing with some of the people at work heightens that feeling. But overall, it doesn't seem more than average. I can handle things pretty well. It might be good to bring this down a bit, but I would always want some challenge, so 10 is okay and 6 or 8 might be better.'

How much do I feel I'm in the right PLACE?

Get close to your feelings about the question; don't try and analyse it. It's a gut response that you need, so that your score is a reflection of that even if you haven't given it any real thought yet.

What does my score for PLACE mean to me?

'I thought this would be higher, because I am pretty happy being at Baines. It's not more because I am still uncertain about my ability to hold down the new job, or even the one I have just come into. It seems too fast a promotion for me to be comfortable. I have to grow into this being my place.'

How much PREJUDICE do I feel against me?

It could be anything from 0 to 20. It's your general feeling right now.

What does my score for PREJUDICE mean to me?

'I doubt if this has ever been so high. I never thought about it before. It's mostly that fear again: that my fellow sales reps don't regard me as their leader and that they, and everybody else at Baines, will think I'm not worthy. I want to get over this.'

How much POWER do I feel I have?

In scoring this, you'll realize straight away that there is no point in comparing your perception and feelings of power with anyone else's. After all, the presidents of the USA and Russia may well put a pretty low score when they grasp what they can't actually do. So your score is based on your own level of satisfaction with yourself.

12

What does my score for POWER mean to me?

'I have been given a lot of power – more than I ever had. I can't make it more than 12 because I hold onto the fear of failure and the concern about people not respecting me. I can make this score much higher. I must be powerful to have been offered this job.'

How much POVERTY do I feel I have?

If you feel poor, give a high score in the range of 0 to 20. If you don't feel poor, give a low score. As always, the meaning is yours, so money could be just a part of any feeling of poverty you may have.

3

What does my score for POVERTY mean to me?

'It has suddenly begun to feel much better financially. My salary and commission have been quite good, but raising two young kids and not having a second income at this point has meant we have struggled to keep up. Now, with my new salary and another significant increase on the way, we will be able to put some away for the children's education and other things for the family. The 3 is because my work keeps me away from enjoying time with my kids as much as I'd like.'

How much PEACE of mind do I feel?

Feel very peaceful inside? Score it nearer the 20 mark. Very little peace of mind for you at this time? Mark it closer to the 0 end of the scale.

10

What does my score for PEACE mean to me?

'I am a bit disappointed with this score. I still worry more than I should. It's back to that fear of failure and not feeling respect that makes it only 10. On the other hand, the 10 is that I do have a sense of being on the right track, and that I do have the trust of my bosses. I look forward to believing in myself more, which will bring me that peace of mind.'

How much PRESSURE do I feel is on me?

It doesn't matter at this stage where you think the pressure is from, or how you deal with it. It has little to do, either, with the actual amount and level of things you have to do or the calls on your time or the requests and expectations others place on you, although they will all add up to something. It's how you feel about those things, on the usual scale of 0 to 20.

13

What does my score for PRESSURE mean to me?

'I have said it, and it seems higher than I thought. Nobody is putting more pressure on me than I am. There is pressure at work from the amount of work and the decisions I have to make, but those are good pressures. They amount to about 3. The rest is about my fear and lack of respect. I can see this is about me, not anyone else.'

After Adam had looked this over, taking in the words carefully, Keith leaned towards him.

'You have clearly come up with your main themes, Adam. Now it's time to put it all together. You have identified your satisfactions and your frustrations and what they mean. These are the positive and negative emotional energies you carry with you at work. Your positive scores add up to 66 and your negative to 41. You already said that you want to change a few things. Next thing is to make a summary of the satisfactions and frustrations. I will leave you a few moments to write them down. If anything has changed as you have talked about them, feel free to change the scores.'

Adam bent his head to his task. It seemed an easy one at this point.

SATISFACTIONS

Note down here the scores that you gave these feelings (they may have changed); then total your scores.

PLEASURE.. 15

PURPOSE.. 17

PLACE.. 12

POWER.. 12

PEACE.. 10

TOTAL.. 66

Satisfactions: the question

Your satisfaction score is the source of your positive energy. You have already made sense of each of the aspects making up your satisfaction. Now you can put all that together and begin to make sense of your total satisfaction in life, as it is at this time.

What does my total score for satisfactions mean?

'My sense of purpose is what is carrying me through a significant change for me. That itself is a change and I am proud of having that purpose. While I am generally happy with my work, I am less sure and less comfortable with my place, my power and my peace of mind. This is due to the transition I am going through and I can change this as I grow into the job.'

FRUSTRATIONS

Write down your frustration scores here and add them up:

PAIN.. 6

PROBLEMS... 10

PREJUDICE... 6

POVERTY... 3

PRESSURE.. 13

TOTAL... 41

Frustrations: the question

Now that you have your total score for the things that frustrate you – your negative energy force – you probably want to compare this with your satisfaction score. Resist the temptation for a short while; don't rush on with your journey too quickly. Always remember that the meaning is more important than the score. The numbers are only there to help you to make sense of things, not to categorize you.

What does my total score for frustrations mean?

'My frustrations are almost all about the change I am going through in my work. It brings up my fear of failure and my sense that others don't, or may not, respect me. This puts pressure on me and that sense of prejudice and having problems that don't really exist.' Adam looked up, his eyes bright. 'You know,' he said, 'I think I know all this, but I never knew I knew it, if you see what I mean.'

'Yes,' said Keith, 'I know exactly what you mean. And now write down the last piece.'

What does my Workscale mean?

From your summaries of your satisfactions and frustration, now consider the essence of all you have shared and write it down here.

'I am in just the place I should be. The transition I am going through has brought up my real feelings and I have to respect them for myself. I can and will make this job a success in the way that I want. It is natural to have fears at this point and I have enough going for me to get through them. As to feeling others are against me, I have no evidence for that, only my own thoughts. My purpose will take me through. And what I am learning here.'

Action

What do I need to do?

'I need to stay on track. I will remind myself daily of my purpose and that I have the ability to carry it out successfully. I will continue to offer my new skills and inspiration to others to help them to be successful.'

What support do I need for this?

'I need the support of my boss and fellow workers. I am happy that my wife really supports and believes in me. And I need the external support of my coach, to help keep me on track.'

It was time for Adam to leave. He scanned his Workscale responses on the train and started making notes. A plan was beginning to emerge, but he had some questions to answer before he could put it into practice. How was he going to introduce the Workscale to his team and to people like Sam? How could he use the Group Dialogue and Learning from Experience tools with them? Could he combine all of this, with Power Listening of course, and become a really effective E-Fitness coach leader? He saw a glimmer of the possibilities. Isn't that what he wanted to have others see: the possibilities? He would talk with Keith about this next time. And he had to respond to Evelyn, who wanted him to run a group session with the leadership team. Meanwhile, he had his sales team to think about, and the targets and the overseas development and the ramping up of their ordering facilities on the internet and the marketing campaign that had to go alongside that. His head started to ache. He sat back for a moment, forced himself to relax, smiled at himself and focused on his purpose. 'I'm in exactly the right place,' he said to himself. 'I'm changing that score from 12 to 20.'

* * * * * *

'Max. Good to see you.' Adam's greeting was genuine. He was always pleased to see Max. They got down to business after the pleasantries.

'I'm getting together with each of the sales reps in the region separately. Gives me a chance to find out more about you all and what I can do to support you the best I can.'

'Good idea,' said Max. 'Never happened before. I've often thought we should do that. Meetings don't give everyone a good chance to talk about the things that they really need to. Not that it stops me,' he added, looking sideways at Adam.

'Right,' agreed Adam. Suddenly he felt a little nervous flutter go through him. 'I want to try something out with you. It's something that I have done and found very useful and I want all the sales team to give it a go. It's called a Workscale and it helps to see where we are satisfied and frustrated in our work.'

'Sounds a bit creepy to me. Still, if you found it useful, I'm game. Can't do any harm, I suppose. Not sure how some of the others will view it.'

'That's why I invited you first, Max. Here's the deal. If you think it's helpful, then I'd like you to back me up when I suggest it to the others. If you don't, I'll give it some more thought.'

Adam gave the Workscale to Max, and asked him to complete the scores.

WORKSCALE

Max

1 How much PLEASURE do I get from my work? .... | 17 |

2 How much PAIN do I have at work? .... | 5 |

3 How much PURPOSE do I have in my work? .... | 15 |

4 How much do PROBLEMS weigh me down? .... | 8 |

5 How much do I feel I'm in the right PLACE? .... | 15 |

6 How much PREJUDICE do I feel against me? .... | 0 |

7 How much POWER do I feel I have? .... | 15 |

8 How much POVERTY do I feel I have? .... | 5 |

9 How much PEACE of mind do I feel? .... | 12 |

10 How much PRESSURE do I feel is on me? .... | 12 |

Total scores (two columns) .... | 74 | | 30 |

'Interesting,' said Max, when he had finished.

'What's interesting?' asked Adam. He was sure Keith would have asked that.

'Well,' answered Max, 'I'm pretty happy with what I do. I was really interested in those last two, though. Not sure about those.'

'Let's go through them one by one. I'm now going to ask you to say what your scores mean to you.'

An hour later, the two of them shook hands warmly. Max was on side. He had also committed to some action steps. He was going to make a note of anything that he saw or anticipated as a problem and he was going to suggest a solution. This he would transmit to Adam. Where it had wider implications, Adam would take it to the person concerned, or to the team if it was appropriate. It seemed that Max had been holding on to the feeling that he, and sometimes he alone, was frustrated by some of the communication and the systems that didn't help the sales efforts. Adam also observed that Max changed some of his scores as he talked. He raised his level of purpose from 15 to 17 and lowered his power from 15 to 13. Max had ideas about what he wanted and he was more ambitious than perhaps either of them had thought.

* * * * * * *

The boardroom had been converted from a corner office and a stock-room last year and was the pride and joy of Marcus Baines. He sat at the head of the table, beaming at the four of them seated in the executive chairs. Andrea fussed around the table, making sure that everyone had notepads and pencils, that water was on the table, the coffee was ready and the blinds at just the right level to avoid the sun from shining into the faces of the people opposite that window. Marcus waited until she had left.

'Good morning,' he began. 'As you know, I will be retiring soon. I haven't made it public yet, and I know you will keep it to your-selves until I do, but this is an opportunity for me to start the process of handing over. Stella, you will remain as director of human re-sources and administration and of course Sam will be here as our operations director. We can officially welcome Adam as our sales director-designate. And, as you know, it's my great pleasure to pass over the reins of managing director to Evelyn. This will take place in five months from today. I've booked my holiday to start the next day.'

He paused for the appreciative laughter and nodding of heads.

'It seems that we are going to throw young Adam into the deep end. Not only is he to take on our sales portfolio, he has also shown interest in helping us to get more with it, so to speak. But I've been told that I mustn't hog this. I'm going to pass it on to Evelyn to tell you more.'

Evelyn was brief. 'Adam has been looking at ways for us to im-prove our communication and I've been very impressed with some of his results so far. I think he has some things that we might find very useful to help us become more efficient and successful at what we do. But if we are to introduce any new methods, I believe that we have to try them out at this level first. So I asked Adam if he would offer us some of his insights. Over to you, Adam.'

Adam took a sip of water; his throat had gone strangely dry. He wondered again if this wasn't going to feel like a conspiracy to Sam. He and Evelyn had discussed what he would do. Evelyn had talked with Marcus about it. Adam had sat down with Stella to go over the Workscale with her. She had been immediately enthusiastic about the possibilities for using it in HR. But nobody had mentioned it to Sam.

Adam spent five minutes outlining what he was going to do. He described the importance of having a healthy balance between the things that satisfied and those that frustrated people at work and the potential results if employees were too frustrated, including sickness, stress, lost time and errors. He talked about the value of listening to those frustrations so that people felt heard and so that they could change them into something more creative and positive. He gave an example from his personal experience: of becoming clearer about his purpose and knowing that when he felt overwhelmed with work, he had to concentrate on what he wanted to achieve.

'Here's an exercise for all of us to do,' he said, and passed around copies of the Workscale. 'I already used it with one of my sales reps and he found it very enlightening. So did I. Please fill in the scores to the questions it asks you.'

It was quiet, apart from the sound of papers being shuffled. Heads were lowered and pencils poised. Numbers were totted up; pencils dropped back onto the table; heads came up to look at Adam.

'This is not a test and the scores you have are not comparable to each other's, since we all have our own perspective on how things are. The only person who knows what your scores mean is you. It's also important for us to agree that whatever we discuss in here is confidential and doesn't leave the room. Is that agreed?'

Four heads nodded. Three of them were smiling; the other had a glum expression on his face.

'Just to get a sense of our differences, tell me what your total scores are – just the two numbers that you have at the bottom.'

'I have 89 and 19,' beamed Marcus and looked around the room. 'Mine are 70 and 33,' said Stella. Evelyn looked at Sam, who had his head down, peering at his scores. 'I have 79 and 38,' she said. Sam looked up, an almost defiant expression on his face. 'I've got 56 and 50,' he intoned.

Adam knew what to do; or at least he knew what not to do. He had talked it over with Keith and was clear that he would not push Sam into talking about his Workscale in the group.

'Thank you all,' he said. 'We'd probably all like to be like Marcus, but we're not – or not yet anyway.' It was, he thought, a weak attempt to work around to where he wanted to be.

'The first score you have is what satisfies you; the second score is what frustrates you. Evelyn and Stella have quite high levels of satisfaction and frustration levels that are manageable. We do need a certain level of frustration to keep us from getting stagnant. Even Marcus has 19, which keeps him creative. Sam, your satisfaction is just a little more than your frustration level, which indicates that things could be a lot better for you. I suggest that you and Evelyn discuss this later. Stella, I wonder if you would be prepared to talk about your scores with us now. The others of us will listen.'

'Certainly,' offered Stella. This was her kind of thing, thought Adam.

Adam held out his hands to the table. 'Marcus, Evelyn and Sam, our job is to listen to Stella and help her to understand the meaning of her scores. So feel free to ask her any questions that help her to make sense of them. We probably don't have time to go through all the scores, but this will give you some idea of how we use the Workscale. Stella, please pick one of those questions out – perhaps one that strikes you as being of special interest – and tell us what it is and what it means to you.'

'I could just start with the first one, but I'm looking at one that seems to be lower than I'd like, if that's okay. I gave 12 for how much power I feel I have. The others on that side are 14 or 16, and I was a bit surprised at this one.'

'Tell us what that 12 represents for you, Stella,' invited Adam.

'Well, I do feel in charge of my little department. We do have some glitches, but we are pretty much on top of things. People always get paid on time without mistakes. I've put a new filing system in place and they are having a bit of a struggle with it, but on the whole we are moving ahead. I'm left to make my own decisions about how HR is run and how the office is organized.'

'Any questions for Stella?' asked Adam.

'Yes.' It was Evelyn. 'You said your 12 was low and a surprise. What's the surprise and what makes it low?'

'When I think about power, I think about being in charge; being in control of things. I feel that I'm not in control of a lot that happens. No, that's not right. I feel that I don't have the time to make the things happen that I want to take place. Like, I really think we should have a good system, a standardized one, of interviewing people, and a far better procedure for regular performance reviews, not to mention having exit interviews.'

'What stops you from setting these things up if they're important?' Evelyn again.

'Just not enough time in the day.' Stella stopped, looked around the room. 'That's not a very good excuse, is it? If I delegated some of the things I'm doing, or if I didn't spend such a lot of my time watching over the others, I could find some time at least to set up a plan.'

'What does that do for your power?' asked Adam.

Stella laughed. 'Make it go up by about 5 points at least.'

'Well done, Stella,' said Marcus. 'And well done, Adam. We should have had these meetings a long time ago. Ah well – at least I can see the future of Baines is in good hands.'

* * * * * * *

Sam came quickly, furtively, into Evelyn's office, shutting the door behind him. He sat on the edge of the chair in front of Evelyn's desk. He held his Workscale between his fingers as though it was too hot to hold.

Evelyn had been well briefed by Adam; and she had seen how he had handled his questioning with Stella, and with Sam the other week.

'I see you have the papers there, Sam. Shall we take a look at those scores and what they mean?'

'I suppose so. Here it is.' He handed the package to Evelyn. She ran her eyes over his scores.

WORKSCALE

Sam

1 How much PLEASURE do I get from my work? ... 12

2 How much PAIN do I have at work? 8

3 How much PURPOSE do I have in my work? 12

4 How much do PROBLEMS weigh me down? 12

5 How much do I feel I'm in the right PLACE? 12

6 How much PREJUDICE do I feel against me? 10

7 How much POWER do I feel I have? 12

8 How much POVERTY do I feel I have? 4

9 How much PEACE of mind do I feel? 8

10 How much PRESSURE do I feel is on me? 16

Total scores (two columns) 56 50

'Well, Sam; we're both new to this, so let's give it a go. Start with that first 12 for how much pleasure you get from your work.'

It took him a little while, but Sam began to warm up once he found that Evelyn was listening to him, not judging him or the scores that he'd put down. If anything, he'd made them look better than he felt at times. By the time they reached the end, he was almost relaxed, nearly allowing himself to smile. Evelyn asked him to read out the final summary statement he had made.

Sam cleared his throat. 'I'm good at my job, and I like it. I am very loyal to Baines. But I've lost my way over the past six months and I've let things get on top of me. I feel that my lack of education has held me back and puts me in a poor light with others. I want to play a full part in this company. I'm going to learn more about managing and I'd appreciate any help I can get.'

* * * * * * *

'Keith,' said Adam. 'This stuff is working.'

Exercise

Now try the Workscale for yourself.

WORKSCALE

Before we start, give a value from 0 to 20 to each of the following 10 questions. For example, if you feel you have a great deal of pleasure from work, give a high score; if you don't feel poverty at all, give a low score; if you feel about halfway on a pressure scale, give about 10 for how much pressure you feel. If you are unsure what a question means, decide on the meaning that makes sense to you.

NAME_____DATE_____

Score each question on a scale 0–20.

1 How much PLEASURE do I get from my work? ... ☐

2 How much PAIN do I have at work? .... ☐

3 How much PURPOSE do I have in my work? .... ☐

4 How much do PROBLEMS weigh me down? .... ☐

5 How much do I feel I'm in the right PLACE? .... ☐

6 How much PREJUDICE do I feel against me? .... ☐

7 How much POWER do I feel I have? .... ☐

8 How much POVERTY do I feel I have? .... ☐

9 How much PEACE of mind do I feel? .... ☐

10 How much PRESSURE do I feel is on me? .... ☐

Total scores (two columns) .... ☐ ☐

How much PLEASURE do I get from my work?

Give a score for that question, on a scale from 0 to 20. The more pleasure you feel you have, the higher the score; the less you feel, the lower the score.

Put your score in this box.

What does my score for PLEASURE mean to me?

How much PAIN do I have at work?

Again, give a score for this anywhere between 0 and 20. Lots of pain will get a high score; little pain will get a low score.

What does my score for PAIN mean to me?

How much PURPOSE do I have in my work?

A great deal of purpose will give you a score towards the 20 mark, very little purpose will have you hovering nearer the 0 point. If you are not sure, or you waver between feeling lots of purpose and not much, you'll probably give a score around the 10 region. Since it's how you feel right now, it has to be right.

What does my score for PURPOSE mean to me?

How much do PROBLEMS weigh me down?

A lot? Give a high score. Not much? Give a low one, on the 0 to 20 scale. Notice that the question isn't about how many problems you have or haven't got; it's about how much you feel they affect you personally and weigh you down.

What does my score for PROBLEMS mean to me?

How much do I feel I'm in the right PLACE?

Get close to your feelings about the question; don't try and analyse it. It's a gut response that you need, so that your score is a reflection of that even if you haven't given it any real thought yet.

What does my score for PLACE mean to me?

How much PREJUDICE do I feel against me?

It could be anything from 0 to 20. It's your general feeling right now.

What does my score for PREJUDICE mean to me?

How much POWER do I feel I have?

In scoring this, you'll realize straight away that there is no point in comparing your perception and feelings of power with anyone else's. After all, the presidents of the USA and Russia may well put a pretty low score when they grasp what they can't actually do. So your score is based on your own level of satisfaction with yourself.

What does my score for POWER mean to me?

How much POVERTY do I feel I have?

If you feel poor, give a high score in the range of 0 to 20. If you don't feel poor, give a low score. As always, the meaning is yours, so money could be just a part of any feeling of poverty you may have.

What does my score for POVERTY mean to me?

How much PEACE of mind do I feel?

Feel very peaceful inside? Score it nearer the 20 mark. Very little peace of mind for you at this time? Mark it closer to the 0 end of the scale.

What does my score for PEACE mean to me?

How much PRESSURE do I feel is on me?

It doesn't matter at this stage where you think the pressure is from, or how you deal with it. It has little to do, either, with the actual amount and level of things you have to do or the calls on your time or the requests and expectations others place on you, although they will all add up to something. It's how you feel about those things, on the usual scale of 0 to 20.

What does my score for PRESSURE mean to me?

SATISFACTIONS

Note down here the scores that you gave these feelings (they may have changed); then total your scores.

PLEASURE................................. ☐

PURPOSE.................................. ☐

PLACE...................................... ☐

POWER..................................... ☐

PEACE...................................... ☐

TOTAL...................................... ☐

Satisfactions: the question

Your satisfaction score is the source of your positive energy. You have already made sense of each of the aspects making up your satisfaction. Now you can put all that together and begin to make sense of your total satisfaction in life, as it is at this time.

What does my total score for satisfactions mean?

FRUSTRATIONS

Write down your frustration scores here and add them up:

PAIN.. ☐

PROBLEMS................................. ☐

PREJUDICE................................. ☐

POVERTY.................................... ☐

PRESSURE.................................. ☐

TOTAL... ☐

Frustrations: the question

Now that you have your total score for the things that frustrate you – your negative energy force – you probably want to compare this with your satisfaction score. Resist the temptation for a short while; don't rush on with your journey too quickly. Always remember that the meaning is more important than the score. The numbers are only there to help you to make sense of things, not to categorize you.

What does my total score for frustrations mean?

WHAT DOES MY WORKSCALE MEAN?

From your summaries of your satisfactions and frustration, now consider the essence of all you have shared and write it down here.

Action
What do I need to do?

What support do I need for this?

Ideally, discuss this with a coach; preferably an E-Fitness coach, or someone who is a good listener.

Inside story
How our emotions shape our image of reality

Preparation

Their summer break had been good. The family had basked in the delights that an Italian village near the sea could offer. Adam felt refreshed and ready to go. The park in late August was bursting with blooms and the weather was warm enough for Keith and Adam to sit on their bench. The fountain now looked smaller and less ornate than Adam remembered, nothing like the genuine Italian ones that he and Pauline had ogled at and the kids had wanted to splash around in. He reflected how easily perceptions changed when you change your experiences.

'I've been thinking,' said Adam. 'I'd like to get together with my sales team and do something different, something energizing that they will really learn from and that will help them to connect more as a team. I also need to prepare for someone to take over as regional sales manager. I have my eyes on Max, but I want to be sure. Any ideas?'

Keith grinned at him. 'As a matter of fact, I do. You remember that I told you about Storytelling? That will fit exactly into what you want to do. It's the fifth and final E-Fitness coaching tool that I am going to show you, although it can often be an excellent introduction to a group, since it leaves them wanting more. We can use it in individual coaching, and you and I will give it a try. Before that, tell me what your thoughts are about what has been happening and what you now think about the possibility of Storytelling in the workplace.'

'As you know, yesterday was my first day back after our holiday, so I had a lot of catching up to do. Although the plant was closed, the sales and technical assistance sides were still there, as well as the admin people. Summer is always a funny time. I had a great meeting with Evelyn. She was so pumped up about Sam and how he was. Mind you, it was only his first day back from holiday too, before all the operatives get back. She said he seemed a different man. Anyway, she told me that she wanted me to come up with a good business argument for bringing in the E-Fitness coaching methods that we have tried out. She is obviously intrigued, but wants to be sure it's not just a fad or something that diverts our attention from our main goals and targets.'

'We will certainly look at that next time, Adam. You might want to start on that and run it by me next week. Meanwhile, do you have any thoughts on Storytelling?'

'I've already given some thought to a business argument and begun to draft something out. I'm not sure how Storytelling will fit into that, but I'm sure to find out. It certainly sounds something that I could try out with the sales team. I'm much more open to the possibilities now that we have done the other work.'

Keith drew out his folder and slipped out two sheets on which were photographs. He handed them to Adam.

'Usually,' said Keith, 'I show the actual objects, but sitting in the park would make that a little impractical. So here are photographs of 10 different objects. Take a look at them and pick one.'

They were everyday items, and some uncommon ones: a pair of old boots, a battery, an old-fashioned egg timer, a stapler, a mobile phone, a small wooden rocking horse, a dictionary, a brass handbell, a half-used candle, and a bar of hand-made soap.

Adam inspected them all. At first, nothing appealed to him more than any other; then as he looked more closely he found that he saw something special in some of them. The boots reminded him of his father, and also of his climbing expedition. The soap reminded him of Pauline's love of natural soap and the stash they had at home, mostly from places they had visited, and still in their wrappers. The rocking horse brought back some old memory that he couldn't quite get to. But it was the egg timer, the sand trickling through its slender waist, that engaged his attention the most. He didn't know why. He pointed to it. 'The egg timer.'

'The egg timer,' repeated Keith, and brought out two more sheets of paper. 'These are blank. I want you to take 10 minutes to write a story. Imagine you are the egg timer. Be as creative as you like and write from the point of view of the egg timer. Tell its story. I'll let you know when you've had 10 minutes.'

Adam was not used to writing, at least not this kind of writing. His pen hovered over the page for what seemed like half of his 10 minutes. Keith said he should be creative and be the egg timer. He let go of his self-consciousness and started.

First story

I was made like this for a very special reason. My very narrow waist and symmetrical shape were honed to a perfect size. The sand that was sealed into me had to be perfect too, in the size of each grain and in the quantity used. Turn me and you will find that the sand runs through in exactly three minutes, time for the perfect boiled egg.

I was made years ago. I was used a lot at first, when the family who owned me regularly had eggs for breakfast. Later I stayed on the shelf and had the indignity of having to listen to that mechanical timer making its ding at the end of its programmed time. Now I seem to have been completely sidelined. I was given away and sit in a box with other old bits and pieces, coming out occasionally as a conversation piece or for someone to pick me out and write a story about me.

What they don't realize is this. Not only am I reliable and will time three minutes every occasion you turn me over, I can also be used as a model for reliable timekeeping for many other purposes. Imagine making another one built to larger specifications. You could have timers like me that will last for five, 10, even 60 minutes. Or more.

Not only that, but I do something that no mechanical, electrical or electronic timer will ever do. I am your visual guide to time passing. It's not for nothing that you talk about the sands of time. I am your reminder that time passes and the only thing you can do about it is to use it as well as you can. I remember in my early days, when I was well used by the family, the little boy used to play with me when his mother wasn't in the kitchen. He would set me on the table and watch my sand trickling through, and then turn me over and watch it all over again. As he grew, he would count and try to get the exact number of seconds, 180, each time. He could only do it when he went a little faster or slower at the end. When he was older, he held his watch up to my side and checked. He seemed satisfied to know that my sand always flowed at exactly the same pace. He tried, but knew he never could, to stop me by sliding me around. He never could stop time. I hope he remembers me.

When Adam finished, Keith asked him to read it out loud. Adam was suddenly glad that they hadn't met in the café. He read his story.

'What do you notice?' asked Keith.

The meaning

Adam looked over it again. For some reason, he was feeling a little emotional. 'I notice I used the word "perfect" three times in the first paragraph. And I notice that the egg timer has a mixture of pride in his ability to be reliable and regret that other people don't use him properly. Also, he suggests how the idea of the egg timer could be used in different ways if there were different sizes. He gets a bit preachy when he talks about the sands of time. Finally there is this little wistful note at the end.'

Keith held his hand up and counted off his fingers as he recited back what he had heard. 'Being perfect; pride in his ability; regret he's not used properly; ideas about possibilities; preachy about an idea; wistful. Do you connect personally with any of those things?'

There was another of those long pauses with which Adam was now familiar and comfortable as he mulled this over.

'All of them, in some way,' he said. 'I don't mean to say that I think I'm perfect; it's more like the circumstances being perfect, as though everything is just in the right place at the right time. In a way, I think that it always is, if only I could see that. I do think that I am reliable. People can count on me to do what I say. Probably I'm the one who doesn't always believe that, and that connects with regretting that others don't always see what I have to offer. To be honest, I think resentful would describe me more; although then again, I can see that it's not even true, only my negative thoughts getting in the way. What else was there?'

'Having suggestions about other possible ways of being used, being a bit preachy and feeling wistful,' said Keith.

'Yes, of course. There's that thing about seeing possibilities again, thinking outside the box and wanting others to see it, which connects with getting kind of preachy. I think that when I do get hold of an idea I tend to want to have others get it too. To be fair to myself, I don't think I do get preachy. It gets back to finding something that inspires me. There's nothing wrong with showing enthusiasm for something you believe in. That's what I really like about Marcus Baines.'

'And the wistful feeling?' prodded Keith.

'Ah, yes. What did I write? "I hope he remembers me." I think I know what that is. It takes me back to my own inquisitiveness as a boy. I was always interested in how things worked, or what they could do. I wasn't aware when I wrote it, but when I read it back I recognized that I was the boy playing with the egg timer. It seems weird, but I want to be sure that I don't leave that enquiring part of me behind.'

'I wonder why you think that's weird. Your inquisitiveness seems to be an important part of who you are. There was something else you wrote about and I haven't heard you mention it. You wrote that the egg timer could do something that no electrical or mechanical, or electronic device could do. I was especially interested since you work for an electronics firm. What does it mean?'

'What does it mean?' repeated Adam slowly. 'Something about its simplicity; and that its very simplicity allows us to see time passing. I'm sure that's what I like about E-Fitness. It's simple, and it works, and it opens up new ways of thinking.'

'That's another valuable insight for you, Adam. Now write down what your story about the egg timer means to you; in other words, what you now understand about yourself.'

Adam bent to his task, and then read back what he had written to Keith.

Keith grinned. 'That was a warm-up,' he said. Now I want you to take another 10 minutes and write a story about something that you have recently observed or experienced at work. Again, write it from your own point of view.'

Second story

Ten minutes later, Adam had written his story. It entailed a series of frustrating conversations he had had with a web designer to upgrade their whole marketing presence on the internet, which eventually turned into a creative and viable solution. Adam noticed the sense of pride he had as he read the story to Keith, and smiled at the recognition.

'I can see how this Storytelling brings out some great information,' remarked Adam. 'My question is, how does it help change things to the extent that it improves our bottom line? I'm all for having something different in our training sessions, but what will we actually get from it?'

'Do you know that quote from Anaïs Nin? "We don't see things as they are, we see them as we are." If you take a look at what you wrote about the egg timer, you can see that you actually wrote about yourself. In your story about the website developer, you wrote about your personal perception of your and her actions. Do you think anyone else would have seen the egg timer, or the conversations you had in the same way and written the same story? Okay, that was a rhetorical question. You know they wouldn't. So what's the lesson here, and what's the point?'

'I know the quote,' Adam replied. 'I have to say, I never really got it. I saw the egg timer not as it is, but as I am. Now that is weird. And I saw the conversations I had with the web developer, not as they were, but as I am. So let me see – that means that what I see as real is just the way I see it. And that means I have to take responsibility for my own perceptions. This is very philosophical.'

'Don't forget that much of philosophy is about values. This one is about accountability, not only for our own actions, but also for the way we see things. You recall how you described Sam as having a negative attitude. What you were getting was that the way he sees things affected his behaviour, which in turn affected others around him. The work of his whole department deteriorated; and it's the most important department in the company. What did he do? He blamed everyone else. When he began to take charge of his own thoughts and actions, and dare I say it, his feelings, things started to turn around. It's early days yet, but if he keeps on this track, just watch how quality and productivity improve over the next few months.'

'I'm not sure I could get Sam to write a story; but I certainly get your point.'

'That's the thing about the different tools I am showing you. If not Storytelling, you have Learning from Experience, or the Work-scale, or the Group Dialogue to choose from. And you will always be using Power Listening. And now,' said Keith, 'let's discuss how you are going to introduce Storytelling to your team.'

The team

Twelve chairs was the maximum that could comfortably be fitted around the boardroom table, and now every chair was occupied. The whole of the regional sales team had responded to his call, and Adam could scarcely contain his delight. The conversation had been animated as they arrived and sipped their coffee or tea and munched on the goodies provided by Andrea. Now they sat looking expect-antly at Adam, their eyes shifting from time to time to the 12 objects on a tray in front of them. There had already been some suggestions. Memory game had been the most favoured, although others were more creative and sometimes ribald.

They knew they were there for a team development training day, and Adam had promised something different. As he described their first exercise, Adam detected a mixture of interest, discomfort, surprise and puzzlement. But nobody demurred, and everybody selected an object. Even the last person had two to choose from.

After the 10 minutes, Adam asked who would like to read their story out. He wasn't surprised when Max volunteered immediately.

'I picked out this rock,' said Max, holding up a fist-sized lump that was shiny on one side, rough on the other and varied in colour be-tween deep brown and a pale mottled pink. 'Here's my story.' And Max began to read.

I was broken from a huge craggy cliff a long time ago. The wind and rain and the waves from the sea in a storm caught me and I fell into the sea, where I remained for many years, half-buried in the ocean floor. The top half became polished and smooth, while my lower part stayed rough.

One day, the tide went out a long way and a child waded out from the beach and found me. He picked me up and took me back to his family,

who admired me. I went home with them. At first I stayed on a shelf where
sometimes a member of the family would pick me up and examine me.
Then the father took me and lowered me into a fish tank. At last
I seemed to have a purpose. The tank was full of tiny fish, different species,
different colours and shapes. Green stuff attached itself to me and food
accumulated on me, so that the fish would come and constantly nudge
me with their mouths, as though they were talking to me, thanking me
for what I gave them. I was happy in there until the disaster.

Fish began to die, floating to the top of the tank. After a while, the
father drained the tank and took me out, where I was examined. It was
pronounced that some of the food sticking to me was contaminated and
I was the cause of the deaths. They cleaned me up and tossed me out
into the garden with other rocks, where I stayed, feeling out of place and
purposeless.

At last, a young man came for me. It was the boy who had first found
me. He had become a geologist and wanted me for his collection. He gave
me a name, a real title, and gave me pride of place with his other specimen
rocks. Now everybody knows me and my history.

As Max put his paper down, a cheer went around the table. Everybody
clapped. As the noise quietened, Adam explained that they were going
to practise asking questions and listening to the response. 'Anyone
like to start by asking Max something about his story?' he enquired.

The questions and the answers flowed, until Adam invited Max to
summarize what he understood from his story, as a result of their
discussion. When he had finished, Max looked at Adam. 'I have to
admit,' he said, 'I thought this was a bit of a joke; something that was
fun but was totally irrelevant. But this is real food for thought. I have
a feeling this is going to change a few things for me.'

Adam asked everyone to move their chairs back so that they had
some space. 'Instead of asking all of you to read your stories out to
the team, I want you to pair up and read yours to one person; and
then ask questions about the story until you have helped the writer
to make sense of it.'

The next half-hour was filled with intense murmurings, occasional
laughter and scribbling. Max sat with Adam, who invited him to say
more about the changes he envisaged.

By lunchtime, the room was buzzing. Afterwards, Adam asked
them all to write down a story of some success they had had at work,

or something they were striving to succeed at. This time they all read their stories to the whole team. The cheers and laughter flowed down the corridor into the offices of Marcus and Evelyn.

'Seems you made quite an impact today,' remarked Evelyn when everyone else had left.

'Well, I hope the impact is going to be felt for a while. Results are what count,' said Adam. 'I'd like to talk with you about my replacement. I've had my eye on Max for a while, and after today I'm convinced he would make a great manager.'

On the way home, Adam leafed through the evaluation responses. The key words and phrases that stared up at him included 'fun', 'eye-opener', 'stimulating', and 'more of this wanted'. He let out a deep breath, realizing that he had not been relaxed at all during the day and thankful that his biggest, unspoken fear had not come about. Nobody had said, 'waste of time'. And they were, he knew, a brutally honest lot.

Reflecting on the day, Adam saw the connections between the E-Fitness coaching tools. He used and, by modelling it, had encouraged others to use Power Listening. Learning from Experience was closely related to Storytelling, and he had used elements of the Group Dialogue. He liked the way he had asked them to write a story of success and wondered what the difference would have been if he had given them a different guideline. The point was, he had been flexible about the way he used the methods. And they still worked. He felt like wrapping his arms around himself in a self-congratulatory hug, but glancing around the train compartment, he thought he might wait until he got home and save it for the kids instead.

Exercise

Try this for yourself. Look at the objects around you. Select one that appeals to you. Pick it up if this is practicable. Check the time. You have 10 minutes to write a story as though you are that object. Do it now, before you read on ...

Bear in mind that you will always gain the most benefit by experiencing all these processes rather than just reading about them. If you have written your story, you can now take a look at it and make sense of it in terms of what it means to you. As with all the E-Fitness tools, nobody but you can make sense of who you are, what you say, how you think or feel. Nobody else but you is the expert on your life. If you take another look at the story that Max wrote, it may be tempting to interpret what he has written. Resist the temptation. Unlike almost any other approach, E-Fitness coaching has at its core the belief that we all have the wisdom we need to be successful in the way we choose, and that the task of the coach is to draw out that wisdom, which often remains concealed until it is drawn out through skilful listening and questioning.

Ultimately, we can become our own best E-Fitness coaches. Until then, it will help if you relate your story to someone whom you trust to listen to you in the way that Keith and now Adam do.

Write down what your story means to you. Is there any action you want to take as a result?

Next, decide who to ask to take part in a Storytelling session. It could be an individual or a group. Everybody has a story. There may be barriers to writing or telling those stories, whether these are language, literacy, disability, lack of confidence, or anything else. People can write in their own language, say their stories, be assured that nobody need hear or read their story if they prefer. Consider the potential barriers to introducing Storytelling and how you will overcome them. The most common barrier to having a successful and productive Storytelling session is the diffidence of the facilitator. How will you overcome your own barriers?

The E-Fitness coach
A self-learning guide for leaders and managers

07

Preparation

The leaves had suddenly fallen, and the grass already glistened with frost. Adam saw his breath plume out in front of him as he walked through the park. They met in the now steamy café, sitting in their usual corner table by the window. The last time he met with Keith, three weeks ago, Adam had reviewed his original learning contract. He'd almost forgotten about it, perhaps, he thought, because he had achieved all he set out to do, and gone beyond it. Having completed the sessions they had agreed, Adam had asked Keith to remain as his coach. Evelyn had approved the payments and had hinted that she might be interested herself. Adam had established a new learning contract for himself.

'Tomorrow is the day,' he told Keith. 'Marcus is going to announce to the company that he is retiring and that Evelyn will be managing director in his place. Evelyn is going to tell everyone that I will replace her as sales director, and I am going to tell the sales department that Max will be the new regional sales manager for the Midlands and Wales. He is over the moon with that.'

'A big day for Baines, then,' remarked Keith, and wasted no time getting down to business. 'Let's see. Your new contract has two major items. The first is for you to generate 20 per cent higher sales by building a highly motivated and competent sales team and at the same time maintaining your own equilibrium. The second is to introduce E-Fitness coaching throughout the company as a way of developing healthy and productive practices.'

'That's right; and we discussed how those are connected, and we also agreed that I can't do that alone. I've already talked with Evelyn and with Stella, who is responsible for HR. They are both interested, but I still have to come up with a business argument. Where do I start?'

'Where would you like to start?'

'Thought you'd say that. I suppose that's what we're paying you for; to ask questions that constantly show us we are in charge and have to make our own decisions and take our own actions. It makes sense for me to start with how I bring in E-Fitness coaching, starting with my own department. It comes down to how I become the kind of leader who inspires others through my coaching style.'

'Very well. In that case, let's explore what you have to do in order to take on that role. You can create your own guide to becoming an E-Fitness coach in your work as sales director.'

In half an hour, Adam had his list. He looked at his watch. He had a meeting at the office and had to leave a little earlier than usual. He'd work on this on the train as always.

The café was becoming busy; the windows steamed up. Adam said, 'When I'm officially sales director next month, I'll have my own office. Let's meet there in future. It's time we stopped skulking around in cafés and park benches, don't you think?'

On the train, he scrolled down his notes, adding to them and noting what he still had to do to prepare himself:

1 Develop a business case (see below).

2 Consult with other directors and managers.

3 Identify clear goals, quantifiable in terms of revenues and savings.

4 Consider the benefits in terms of improved working practices and health.

5 Demonstrate how E-Fitness coaching tool will help meet our targets.

6 Meet with Evelyn and Stella (and Sam?).

7 Make proposal for one year (and get it approved).

8 Introduce E-Fitness tools to leadership group.

9 Introduce E-Fitness tools to sales managers.

10 Discuss with Stella how to introduce to other departments.

11 Train sales (and other?) managers in Power Listening and Group Dialogue.

12 Demonstrate the use of the Workscale and Learning from Experience.

13 Run Storytelling sessions with different teams.

14 Measure results in relation to goals as identified.

A business case

Adam had talked with Keith about some of the points that he wanted to make in building a business case. Now he made his notes.

1 Baines Electronics has a goal over the next 12 months to expand its sales and output by 20 per cent. This is a significant increase which will place big demands on an already busy sales staff and stretch the resources of the operational departments and administrative support services. While there is some allowance for additional operational staff, albeit mainly part time, there is little additional working space without moving or finding an external building. The implication is that we are seeking to expand without much in the way of additional resources. This proposal will provide the motivation and increase the skills of sales staff, improve communication within and between teams and generate ideas for improved practices.

2 Current working practices indicate a higher than acceptable level of rejected goods reach the final stage of production, that returns are commonplace and that delivery dates are frequently compromised. The causes for this have been unclear, but from the few experimental E-Fitness coaching practices that have been used, early indications are that poor communication and personal dissatisfaction, plus stress, are equally common. E-Fitness coaching will provide managers and employees at all

levels with the skills and tools needed for healthy, productive and effective work.

3 The connection between an individual's state of emotional fitness and performance is indisputable. This can be seen from the world of sport (Tiger Woods) as well as in large corporate entities (the Clapham Junction train disaster), and even the stock market crash and eventual demise of many financial institutions. We have already demonstrated that the use of E-Fitness coaching tools has had short-term benefits on the individuals and the teams we have worked with.

4 The hoped-for and predicted outcomes for Baines Electronics over the next year through engaging E-Fitness coaching methods are as follows:

– an increase of 20% in sales;

– a reduction of 15% in returns due to poor quality;

– a reduction of 10% in staff turnover, now standing at 15% full time and 20% part time;

– a decrease in wastage of 10%;

– a faster production cycle, reducing delivery times by 15%.

5 The above can be quantified in terms of pounds and pence. The estimated total due to increased revenue and savings amounts to over £25 million. Taking into account the additional costs for labour, machinery and the time taken for training and material, the growth in profits comes to more than £12 million; an increase over last year of about 50%.

Adam looked back over this. He didn't believe it. Either his sums or his optimism were out of line. What had he missed – or overestimated? He'd go back over it and discuss it with Keith. In any case, he wanted to check with Evelyn to see if she thought he was on the right lines. It didn't have to be perfect before the final proposal, and she would want some input anyway. He'd get the exact figures from Stella and work out the percentages again. She would know the formula.

Pitfalls and objections and how to overcome them

Stella wasn't making it easy for him. He'd thought that she would be enthusiastic; after all, she had said that she had wanted to do this kind of thing. She had welcomed him into her office; she had listened to him, and she said she had some questions and would play devil's advocate. But it gradually seemed to him that her questions were more attacking than he had anticipated.

'This looks like a big task, Adam; especially when you are just moving into a new and highly responsible position. How are you going to have time for this?'

'It's more a matter of style, as I see it,' Adam answered. 'For example, I don't see that there are going to be more meetings than we already have, but they would be very different. And instead of the regular reports and assessment and appraisal procedures that we now have, I would utilize coaching techniques. Also, I would train the sales managers to work with their teams differently.'

'And how,' enquired Stella, with a smile that belied her tone and her eyes, 'do you know that you have the skills to do that? As far as I know you've been in sales for several years; and only recently in a management position.'

Adam felt some heat at the back of his neck. 'That's true, but I've learned a whole lot from my coach in the past few months.'

'Keith Parkinson, I believe. It never struck me that he was very well qualified either in that respect.'

Now he felt his face flush. 'He was my boss, if you remember. You would hardly know that he was the same man. This E-Fitness coaching has really changed him. And me too. We are living examples of the possibilities.'

Stella ignored this. Suddenly, Adam caught the now blindingly obvious fact that he was doing something that Stella believed she should be doing, not him. She saw him as taking on her job, and she didn't like it one bit. He had blundered into this. Meanwhile, another question was coming at him.

'Now let's look at your estimate of results. How on earth are you going to get everyone on side and how are these methods going to have the outcomes you anticipate inside a year?'

'Yes, I think there's a real hole in my thinking here. It's probably where I need the most help. What have I missed?' How could he gain her support? Was it too late?

'There's a hole all right,' she said. 'It looks as though you have assumed everyone in Baines will be engaged in this changed approach in the next few weeks for this to happen. Do you know how long change takes, and how much resistance you'll get?' And before Adam could respond, she continued. 'And when are people getting on with their real work while they are telling stories and listening to each other talk about their woes?'

He felt as though he had just received a blow to the stomach and an uppercut to the chin. Was he out for the count? Stella's phone rang. She smiled sweetly at him and answered it. Saved by the bell. And, just like the prize fighter in those old films who scrabbles for the corner and whose coach throws a bucket of cold water over him to revive him, Adam imagined Keith asking him, 'What happened to everything we talked about?' and Adam answering, 'I forgot it all. I'm not listening to her.' He bounced off the ropes just as Stella put the phone down.

'Sorry for the interruption,' said Stella, 'I told them not to call unless there was an emergency. It seems there's always one. Another employee who is having a crisis and walked off the line. I'll have to go down there in a few minutes. Now, where were we?'

'Stella, I think that you are telling me I am going about this the wrong way, and I agree with you. I let my enthusiasm run away with me. Can we start again? I know you don't have time right now, but I'd like to come back later and ask you how you see things. I'm on a very steep learning curve, and your experience is going to be crucial in helping us to make the changes we need in order to reach our targets.' Had he overdone it? Thank goodness he hadn't made a remark about the employee crisis.

'This should take about 20 minutes; and then I have a meeting to go to and a call with the union official. How about later this afternoon?'

He was back at four o'clock. The breathing space had been vital. He still wasn't sure quite where to start. He just knew he had to listen to her. He'd begin with a question.

'How did it go this morning with that employee?'

Stella looked intently at him. 'The usual,' she said. 'Ruffled feathers – something the supervisor said that he claims she misunderstood. May be true; she hasn't been here long from Romania and her English is a little basic. She thought he told her she wasn't working hard enough and he said he'd asked if she could put in some extra time. Anyway, it seems to be sorted. I left Maria to do some mediation. She's excellent at that.' Again, she looked sharply at Adam.

'I've been thinking about what you were asking earlier,' he said. 'It would be really helpful for me to understand more about your concerns. I know that I don't have all the answers, but at least I'd understand the issues. You asked me about change and how long it takes, and the resistance to it. Could you say more about that?'

'Nobody likes change. We are creatures of habit. If you try to institute something that is different in a short space of time, you are bound to have resistance. For a start the union would be down on us if we don't consult with them, and if we do it takes for ever.'

'How do you go about change?'

'Slowly and carefully,' said Stella. 'Look, Adam; I know you are very keen and I don't want to dampen your enthusiasm, but do take care not to rush in with that new broom. You might find that you sweep away more than you bargained for.'

'I can see that. I have two questions. Given that we have a target for significant growth, what do you think are the things we have to change?'

'We certainly have to change some practices to become more efficient. Actually, your points about quality and wastage and staffing are good ones. Frankly I'd rather spend more time on implementing better employee practices than putting out fires all the time. I know that Sharon and Maria are both very keen to look at how we can improve our recruiting and orientation procedures, but it's hard to find the time with our current resources.'

'So, for example,' said Adam tentatively, 'what could have prevented today's little crisis from occurring?'

That look again. 'Things happen, you know,' Stella said. 'The problem there was communication. It's often one of the supervisors who put their foot in it. We'd have to get them to take more care that they are understood; or teach them Polish and Romanian and whatever other languages their staff speak.'

Adam laughed. 'Failing that,' he said, 'you would like them to communicate better.'

'It would certainly help. You've no idea how much time it takes to put things right after they've gone wrong. The problem is that most of our supervisors came off the line. They have good practical skills, and they are very loyal to Baines, but it's rare to find one that is a good people person. Even most of the department managers rose up through the ranks, as it were. Come to that, so did Sam. He's an example of how we built Baines: people who have been around a long time being promoted. The operatives know that their director was once one of them and that's positive. The trouble is that we've grown to the extent that we no longer have that family feel, and managers and supervisors don't quite understand about communicating with their staff, or each other.'

Adam was silent. He waited.

Stella broke. 'In a sense, I can see that what you want to do is what we need. My suggestion is that we do a trial run; say work with a few selected teams at different levels. We always have to start at the top; get people on board who are going to make the decisions; then one of the management groups, then pick a few operational teams and of course your salespeople. You should probably go with them before taking it to the others. After all, you must be more comfortable with them. Then, instead of trying to do this with everyone, look at, say, a cross section of 10 per cent. You could even ask for volunteers.'

'Will you help me?'

The look again; but it was softer, lingered longer. 'I'll see what I can do,' she said. And smiled.

What happened

The seasons moved on. The seventh monthly newsletter was already out. It had been one of the innovations suggested at an early Group Dialogue session. Andrea and Maria had leapt on the idea avidly, had recruited an editorial board of employees and several keen photographers. Adam read it greedily on the train home.

Employee of the month was Alicia Bratianu for her idea on streamlining the movement of finished goods to the warehouse. It had saved 20 minutes each day and meant less handling and potential damage.

When the procedure was transferred to all of the lines and successfully implemented, someone in finance estimated the savings to be nearly £1 million every year. Alicia would be receiving a bonus, along with her team for supporting her.

There was a photograph of Matthew, with a caption describing how he had come up with a more efficient way to deal with maintenance requests that was bound to keep everyone happy. Matthew certainly looked happy in the photo.

Stella had written an article outlining a scheme to bring out the talent of employees and to create a method of succession planning to allow more people the chance of promotion and offering educational opportunities. She finished by thanking Andrea, Sharon and Maria for stepping up to take on some of Stella's work, giving her a chance to concentrate on people development, as she called it.

A picture of Sam holding one of the new GPS navigators to come off the line took up half a page. With him were the designer, the department manager and the supervisor, with the team in the background. Sam was smiling. Adam smiled back at the photograph. It had taken a couple of difficult Group Dialogues and several conversations with Evelyn before Sam began to show the confidence and skills to open up his communication with the designer and with his own managers. There was still a long way to go, but successes like this one would help.

Adam felt the greatest pride in the double-page spread that featured Max and his regional sales team, shown at the end of a two-day retreat they had organized. Maria had conducted an interview with Max, in which he talked about the successes of the team, and how he attributed it to the way they had perfected the art of listening. 'We really hear what the customer wants now,' he was quoted as saying. The article also commented on the three-way joint communication and learning network between sales, operations and customer technical support that had been established. 'It's been a fantastic help,' said Max. 'We've learned a lot about each other's work and how we can provide the best service we can to each other in the interests of the customer, and therefore Baines Electronics. That's all of us.'

As usual, Adam turned finally to the piece by Evelyn. Instead of the usual shot of her taken sitting at her desk, she was shown on the shop floor with some of the operatives, in front of the photograph on the wall of Trevor and Marcus Baines. The two founders.

'At the end of this month,' Evelyn began in her article, 'I will have been the head of this remarkable firm for one year. It hardly seems possible. This business, started 47 years ago by my father and my uncle, is hardly recognizable today, except in two respects. We still make quality equipment that people want; and we are still a family business. Perhaps even more today, we are a thriving and successful family, even if we come from different backgrounds and countries. You have all helped me to learn to be a better leader here.

'Coming from such a different industry, I felt ill prepared to take on this task. I have Marcus Baines to thank first of all for encouraging and persuading me that I could do this. However, I discovered I could only do this job if I relied on the people around me to do theirs. Learning to trust and learning to delegate with confidence have not been easy. But they have paid off handsomely.

'When I look around, step into any department, watch people at work on the line, or listen in to a sales conference, something wonderful is taking place. People are supporting each other. They take the time to listen. Underneath the usual conversation, Baines employees keep their eyes open to the possibilities. They wonder how to improve things, how they can offer a better service. Team meetings have become so productive that we can hardly keep up with all the ideas. Bear with us; we in management are also learning and sharing great ideas.

'On that note, I owe an enormous debt of gratitude to my fellow directors, Stella Oxberry, Sam Chandler and Adam Bender. Stella and Adam have been instrumental in helping us to become better leaders. Adam has brought an injection of energy and skills that extends far beyond the bounds of his department. Sam, as he has for many years, has shown us his adaptability. This year has perhaps brought about the biggest change, not this time with technical innovation, but with different management techniques.

'Finally, we are on track with the growth that we set ourselves. This is taking place in difficult and unpredictable economic circumstances. The reason is because we are working together, listening to each other and supporting each other through sometimes challenging circumstances. Thank you and congratulations to you all.'

The train arrived at Adam's home station. He turned up the collar of his coat and hurried through the park. He lingered a while at the fountain. Evelyn hadn't referred to some of the difficulties, but after all they had been easily outweighed by the benefits. Getting Stella on side so that she and he partnered on this project had been brilliant. He wondered why Evelyn hadn't mentioned Keith. After all, he had really been the spark that had helped get them where they are. On the other hand, thought Adam, that's what happens to E-Fitness coaches. They get themselves out of the way, so they tend to get left out. Lucky they're emotionally fit. And lucky, mused Adam, that he's still my coach.

Exercise

Consider your own situation. How will you go about bringing Emotional Fitness into the workplace environment?

First, answer a few questions about your circumstances:

1 What is your role now?
2 Do you see your role changing in any way? If so how?
3 Which organization are you in (or do you want to focus on)?
4 What are the main three issues facing the organization?
5 What do you believe needs to be changed?
6 How do you think E-Fitness coaching can assist in these changes?

Next, consider the preparation that Adam made. What do you need to think about?

1 Write down a preliminary draft of your business case.
2 Who do you need to consult with in or outside the organization?
3 What are your clear goals, quantifiable in terms of revenues and savings?
4 What will be the benefits in terms of improved working practices and health?
5 How can you demonstrate how E-Fitness coaching tools will help meet targets?
6 Who do you need to get on side?
7 How will you introduce E-Fitness tools to the leadership?

8   What will you need from a team and who will be on it?

9   Complete your business case.

10 Design a one-year programme and the strategy for carrying it out.

11 How will you introduce E-Fitness tools to other key players?

12 How will you measure results in relation to goals as identified?

Actions speak louder

Now you know, what do you do?

A practical primer on setting up and maintaining an E-Fitness programme

Whatever your role is in your work, you can be an Emotional Fitness coach. Whether you are a manager or an aspiring one, or have any kind of leadership position as the head of a large company or the supervisor of one staff member, you can utilize E-Fitness coaching to great effect. Your leadership style and the skills you have, together with the tools that E-Fitness brings to your coaching or mentoring, define your ability, not the actual role or title you have. Naturally, the greater influence and decision-making authority you have within an organization, the greater is your ability to make the changes needed to bring about healthy and productive working practices. Using the tools of E-Fitness coaching will add to your influence.

Having read, and hopefully worked through and practised, the skills and tools of Emotional Fitness outlined in this book, you are ready to take the next steps. You are none of the characters described here. Adam and Keith, Evelyn and Marcus and the rest are composites of people with whom I have worked over the past 30 years. Perhaps you recognize some of them in the people you know, or within yourself. Now it is time for you to put your own individual stamp on the approach.

Preparation

In one word, your preparation is to practise. To make it three words; practise, practise, practise.

Practise with friends and family, colleagues and acquaintances; anyone who is willing to give you time to try out any of these tools. Practise Power Listening anywhere you go, with anybody at any time; with customers or the car park attendant, with shop staff and your neighbour; with your children and their teachers; with those you like and dislike. Afterwards, note down the responses and the changes; what went well and what you could improve. Make no assumptions on going in to a Power Listening conversation, except that the person wants to be listened to. Check your conversation afterwards with the five Power Listening stages. You will find that it seldom runs smoothly through each stage. Rather, you may set up a contract (even in your own mind), find that the person identifies and focuses on a topic and then, when you attempt to clarify it, moves away from that onto something else. If it was important, they will come back to it. If not, then you move to clarifying what they now talk about. When you summarize it back to them, they might change it, so you can go back to the beginning and set a new contract. The important thing to remember is that without each of the first four stages, you are unlikely to help the talker to discover their own workable action.

Practise Learning from Experience with two or three people, noting afterwards the impact and the insights that took place and how you might develop your skills in using this tool, as well as considering where and with whom it would be most relevant.

Practise the Group Dialogue with a group of at least three other people, or at the most 12. Do this three or four times until you are comfortable facilitating and have also encouraged and witnessed someone else facilitating, under your guidance. The group could consist of family members, friends, work colleagues, sports teams or any group of individuals who would commit to spending an hour or two trying something out. Once again, note how this went and what was learned and how you could improve on your facilitation of the Group Dialogue.

Practise the Workscale, perhaps with some of the same people with whom you have already tried the other tools. Give time for this; you often need more than one session. Be prepared for anything that gets thrown at you. The most valuable part of this tool is the way that you can help people see, understand and own the connections between the different aspects of their satisfactions and frustrations. Note that you can use the Workscale at different times with the same person, which is when you, and that person, see the tangible changes that have taken place. The Workscale is a highly effective barometer of how people feel about themselves and their work. Imagine using the Workscale with different teams across an organization. You will discover the relative emotional health of those teams, which is when you can look for the variables and see what adjustments are needed.

Practise Storytelling, either with individuals or with a group of people. Practise combining some of the tools. Never stop practising. Write down the changes that you notice taking place. When you are satisfied that you have seen and experienced some positive changes, you are ready to take the next step.

Starting out

You may have decided what you want to change before even picking up this book, but this is the time to review your purpose and goals. Note your answers to the following questions:

1 What changes do I want to see?
2 What is the need and how is it expressed?
3 Who are the primary people I want to coach?
4 Who are the others players?
5 What is my role and how can I best use it?
6 How will I know when I have achieved my goals?
7 How will I measure success so that others see it?
8 What is my timeline?
9 What support do I have, and what do I need?
10 What other questions do I need to answer?

Establishing agreements

The predeterminant of success for the implementation of an E-Fitness coaching programme is the same as for Power Listening. It is the establishment of the agreement, or the contract.

Once you are clear about the answers to the questions in the previous section, you can go about establishing those agreements. First, define who your coaching clients are and what the contractual relationship is. When you step into your E-Fitness coaching shoes, be aware that they are your clients, whether they are your employees, your customers, your bosses or your colleagues.

Second, be prepared to describe openly and fully what you are offering, what the limitations are, the length of time or number of sessions, whether this is in person or at a distance, and the ethical values on which you base your coaching. As for the last, you can do no better than adhere to the ethical guidelines laid down by the International Coach Federation. Becoming a member of the ICF and preferably gaining or working towards an accreditation awarded by that professional body will be an advantage in working with any organization, either as an internal coach or as an externally hired coach.

Third, use the Power Listening approach to help the person to establish their own goals and make sure that they and you write them down. Draft out your own form of contract so that both or all parties are clear about what is to be offered and desired, including any fees and time commitments.

First sessions

The contract-setting stage actually sets the scene for the way you will be working, so that the client is already aware of and has experienced a valuable Power Listening session. The first session or two after that are the ones that will almost certainly have the most impact, since it will probably be the first time that the client has felt listened to so intently and in such a focused and purposeful way.

Those early sessions will also enable you to determine what the major themes or issues are and which of the E-Fitness tools you may be using. You are always going to use Power Listening, but you can discern what else will be helpful. Here are a few pointers.

Does the person exhibit a lack in confidence in their own abilities? Learning from Experience could be a valuable tool to use here. The aim here is to help them to see that what they bring is valuable and also an encouragement for them to take control of their own continuous learning and development.

Does the person seem negative, perhaps stuck? Is there some indication of stress or imbalance? The Workscale is an ideal tool to use. It draws out the key issues and, more significantly, empowers the individual to make the changes they need in order to move from frustration to more positive action and, almost inevitably, greater satisfaction and motivation.

Are there issues within a team that show the need for better communication? Don't hesitate to offer the Group Dialogue as a way forward. As the E-Fitness coach, whether your official role is as mediator, facilitator, manager or human resource professional, your job is not only to run a session, but also to guide other members of the team to become facilitators of the Group Dialogue.

Does the person you are working with fall naturally into the telling of stories, without seeing their significance? Do they have a tendency to blame others for the things that go wrong, or sit back and let others take the initiative rather than seeing themselves as someone who could? Try a Storytelling session.

You will learn which tool or combination of tools will be the most appropriate for different circumstances. And remember that the most effective coaches have a coach of their own, and the most effective E-Fitness coaches have an E-Fitness coach to turn to.

Evaluation and feedback

Decide how you will evaluate your work as an E-Fitness coach and receive feedback (as well as give it). There are three reasons for instituting an evaluation procedure:

- It is often hard to assess the actual progress a person is making. However well or poorly they appear to be responding within your sessions, the only real indicator is how well or poorly they perform in their work (or any other) setting.

Depending upon your own role and circumstances, and the extent to which you are able to observe their work practices, you might need variable ways to evaluate their progress. The evaluation needs to be an integral part of the initial contract.

- The harder it is for you to see the actual results, the more important it is for you to receive information about the progress and the achievement of the goals originally set, both by the person being coached and the impact of their behaviour on the overall goals of an organization.

- Coaching can often be an isolated profession. This is ironic, given the fact that you are working closely and intensely with people. The nature of E-Fitness coaching is such that, since you are keeping yourself out of the way, you may not automatically hear about the progress people make. In order to maintain their own levels of enthusiasm and motivation, E-Fitness coaches need to receive the feedback that tells them how they are doing. While I can guarantee you that these processes actually work, you won't always know that unless you ask for the evidence that demonstrates the desired changes.

Measuring the impact of E-Fitness interventions

There are two kinds of measurements: quantitative and qualitative. Because it is easier to measure hard data – increased revenue or profit levels, reduced costs due to improved staff retention, for example – it is tempting to ignore the harder to measure but equally important soft information. How do we measure an atmosphere at work that has changed from stressful to encouraging? Why is it useful to know that one department head is regarded as approachable while another is seen as obstructive? What value can we put on emotional fitness in relation to the success of an organization?

Take another look at the organizational E-Fitness questionnaire at the end of Chapter 1. The questions there can all be turned into measurements of the impact of E-Fitness coaching. Most of them are about the quality of experience that people have from the organization. All of them, in turn, may be transformed into quantitative data, since there are a cost and a benefit attached to E-Fitness. We have already seen how the lack of listening, understanding and commensurate action can cost lives, not to mention incur huge financial losses. On the other end of the scale, an organization, and the people in it, displaying a positive, healthy outlook brings greater success in the short and the long term.

Jack Layton, a fine Canadian political leader who died in 2011, expressed it well in a final letter he wrote to the Canadian public before he succumbed to cancer. 'My friends,' he wrote, 'Love is better than anger. Hope is better than fear. Optimism is better than despair. So let us be loving, hopeful and optimistic. And we'll change the world.'

Consider how you will measure the current levels of love relative to anger, hope relative to fear, and optimism relative to despair in the individuals and organizations you work with. What would be the benefits of changing them?

The Workscale is a measurement of one person's level of positive and negative emotional energy and can be used across a team or organization to see the aggregate level of what that balance is.

As you make use of the tools of E-Fitness, you will start to accumulate your own store of information and wisdom about the efficacy of the approach and the resultant impact. This will be invaluable to you as you continue to develop the practice and spread it to others.

Integrating E-Fitness coaching into management practices

You don't have to be a coach to use these E-Fitness tools. In fact, the best way to see results is to integrate them into your natural, normal way of doing things as a business leader, manager or professional. E-Fitness coaching is a style, not a role. If you are the kind of manager who sees that role in terms of mentoring or facilitating others, then this approach will fit exactly. Rather than E-Fitness coaching being an add-on, devise ways of integrating it seamlessly into the way you do things now.

Use it in interviews, in appraisals, in team meetings, in project discussions, in your regular review or planning sessions. Use it when talking with customers, having conversations at coffee breaks, at disciplinary meetings, board discussions, retirement parties. When you use it on those and other occasions, it will become second nature to you, expected and appreciated by others and, eventually, part of the culture of an organization. You may not change the world, but you will change your corner of it.

Building support for the E-Fitness coach

The real training and preparation to become an E-Fitness coach are to experience the process and apply it to yourself first. It is axiomatic that you cannot take people where you have not been yourself, nor is it ethical to do so. The implication of this is that you become more self-aware, have greater inner resources and resilience, and have a positive outlook. In other words, you become more emotionally fit. Having said that, none of us ever gets to a state of perfection. In doing this work, all of us need support.

Start building your own support structure from the beginning. Who will you invite to be your own coach? Can you establish your own support group where you can take your turn to present your topics in Group Dialogue sessions?

You may link into the Emotional Fitness Institute, where you can connect with other E-Fitness coaches, or read some of the other books about Emotional Fitness. You could set your own E-Fitness coaching support group up in your own location or online.

For more general coaching support, investigate the ICF or other professional coaching associations in your location and consider joining them. The British Association of Counselling and Psychotherapy (BACP) now has a coaching section, which may be right for you. Check out some of the contacts in the back of this book.

Are you having fun yet?

This is a serious question. When you find yourself having fun because you are using the tools of E-Fitness and seeing the results, you know that something is working. That is not to negate the previous discussion about measurements, rather to acknowledge that after all, and in line with the whole philosophy of Emotional Fitness, when you are enjoying yourself and what you are doing, you know you are being productive and successful.

How do you answer the question? Are you having fun yet? Yes; no; maybe?

Now answer this: what brings you, or could bring you, the most fun at work?

When you have answered that question, go right back to Power Listening to get to the essence of what your answer means, and then to the action you need to take.

Spreading the E-Fitness bug
How to make it viral

Don't keep it to yourself: the value of sharing the benefits

The flight had been the longest he had ever taken. But not gruelling, thought Keith Parkinson as the big jet approached Melbourne Airport. He had slept when he'd needed, worked when he wanted, talked with his fellow passengers when the mood took them. All he wanted was some exercise once he had settled into his hotel and he would be ready for the conference the next day.

He was looking forward to it, and especially to the session he was giving on Emotional Fitness to the delegates at the Australasian International Coach Federation Conference. This was a challenge that he had given himself and he noticed the mixture of nervous energy and excited anticipation that was for ever present with him on this journey. He had Adam's agreement that gave him the permission he requested to use the example of Baines Electronics in his presentation.

It was mid morning by the time Keith arrived in Melbourne. He gave himself the afternoon to get his bearings and wander around, discovering the friendly and easy bus system, including the tram car. After a good rest, he made his way to the conference centre. He met coaches from all over the world, although most of them were from Australia and New Zealand. They were life coaches, business coaches, executive coaches, coaches who specialized in certain approaches. Some had been coaching for several years; others were just entering the profession. Some worked on contract or had private practices, others were coaches inside their organizations, or were human resource professionals who offered coaching. All were equally enthused about coaching and its potential impact.

The following afternoon, Keith stood in front of nearly 100 people who had squeezed into the room designed for 80 and had chosen to come to his seminar on E-Fitness coaching. He had only 90 minutes, and he wanted to make it an enlightening and positive experience for them. He began unconventionally, asking them to think about what had attracted them to attend this session and then engaging in a coaching conversation with the first three people who responded, using Power Listening.

When the session was over, people crowded around him, seeking books, more information about training, or how to incorporate E-Fitness into their coaching practices. Adam's story had enthused them, as well as a brief experience of trying out the Workscale with each other in the session.

On the flight home to England, Keith flipped through his notes and the business cards that he had been showered with. The notes were a random collection of thoughts that he planned to put into some order as soon as he got home. They were a combination of the story that he had told about Adam and the feedback and questions he had received from the conference delegates.

1 Adam – sensible to develop a pilot programme for a year rather than going full steam ahead even if it meant reducing his goals to more realistic levels and engaging about 10 per cent of employees in the initial project.

2 Bringing in a support team of key people to manage and evaluate the programme was essential to its success.

3 Starting with the leadership team was another vital element, as was the selection of a cross section of teams and individuals who would receive the coaching on a voluntary basis.

4 Training the team leaders and supervisors to facilitate Group Dialogue and coaching them through the first two or three meetings proved to be crucial.

5 Anybody who expressed doubts or was critical of the programme was allowed to opt out.

6 Results were monitored consistently and at the end of 12 months were considered wildly successful.

7 Plans have been made to train all managers in E-Fitness coaching and to integrate the approach fully.

8 Requests from 35 people at the ICF Australasian conference for follow-up.

As Keith dozed off, he pictured the impact of Baines's success reaching the other side of the world. If only 10 of those at his seminar chose to do something about it, thousands of people in dozens of organizations could reap the benefit before the end of another year.

Developing a wider vision

Evelyn Baines-Young lifted her glass and surveyed the crowded room, packed with employees.

'I want to propose a toast,' she said, once the hubbub of a thousand conversations had died down. 'To the remarkable people who have made Baines Electronics such a success story. To all of you.'

The din that greeted her was a mixture of cheers, laughter and clapping. She put down her glass, looked around again.

'Three years from now we will be celebrating our 50th anniversary, but I didn't want to wait until then to honour our founder and recently retired leader, Marcus Baines.' More cheers and prolonged clapping as Marcus stood up, bowing slightly. 'Before my uncle left us to take some well-deserved relaxation, like building a new sun lounge –' (laughter...) '– he left us with a wonderful legacy. First he passed on a wealth of experience and a sound company making innovative and excellent products. Second, it was in his last few months at the helm that he approved what has become a programme to take us into a new era and another half-century of prosperity, no matter what the doom-and-gloom economic pundits tell us. (clapping and ironic cheering...)

'We have started on a track from which we will not turn. Your engagement in helping us to form ideas and make changes for the better has proved enormously valuable. Your feedback, helping us to put things right where there were faults, has saved money and much heartache. Your willingness to take the initiative even beyond your own lines of responsibility has brought new business, raised our standards and improved our profits. I hope that you feel your efforts have been worthwhile, and that our bonuses and profit-sharing schemes have reflected your contributions. There is more to come. (sustained cheering and clapping...)

'Now I want to look ahead. Our business is no different from any other in that its prime purpose is to make a profit. But this is not our only purpose and I want us to be different from other companies in one very important respect. We are creating a company that truly listens to our employees, to our customers and to our community. That may not sound much until you realize how hard that really is, and that we are actually doing it. Over the next year, and for the foreseeable future, we will be bringing in systems and the support that goes with them to ensure that everyone is heard, that everyone's views and suggestions are valued and that each one of us has the opportunity to learn from what goes on here. Hierarchy will be less important than personal responsibility. Respect will be given to all and expected from all. When things go wrong, we will learn from the experience. When things go right, we will share the stories. When there is any dissatisfaction, we will help you to make the changes needed. The success of each person contributes to the success of us all; therefore our task is to help each other to be successful.'

Evelyn sat down amid tumultuous applause.

Becoming an E-Fitness instructor

'If you'd asked me a year ago,' confided Stella Oxberry to Andrea, 'I would never imagine that I would be teaching people how to be mentors and coaches. Taking that training has given me a load of new energy. Frankly, I was getting a bit jaded with the same old, same old at work.' The director of Human Resources and administration for Baines Electronics gave a rueful smile. 'I just wish that I'd taken this on years ago.'

'How could you?' asked Andrea. 'There never seemed to be any time. What really happened?'

'Well, you know when Adam started to do some coaching, and then tried out a Group Dialogue with your team, I was interested, but it wasn't until I really experienced it that I saw how E-Fitness could have an enormous impact on all of us. Adam was just getting into his job as sales director and wasn't sure how he was going to do the training, so I suggested that I take it on. That meant I had to go and get trained myself first.'

'What did you have to do?'

'First I took the training to become an E-Fitness coach. You know there are more tools to learn when you get the full certification, which allows you do life coaching. The ones we use are designed for business. Anyway, after that I had to go on another course to help facilitate; which is when I really learned a whole lot more to get my E-Fitness Instructor certificate. Now I'm ready to bring it into Baines. I'm going to start with the regional sales managers, then the operational managers.'

'How long did it take you to get trained?'

'About a year; but I began to use it almost immediately, so I knew it was working.'

'And how are you going to find the time to do all that training and still do everything you do?'

'First of all, I have become so good at delegation that much of what I did before is taken care of by the others. The other thing is that, as I do the first phase of training with the management teams, I will be on the lookout for potential instructors. They will do the rest. We have a three-year plan to get all our E-Fitness practices in place. That's in line with our business development plan. One won't happen without the other.'

'You're certainly looking good, Stella. I can't remember when you've seemed so bubbly.'

Talking about E-Fitness

On the three or four occasions that Adam had attended Chamber of Commerce meetings, he had found them somewhat stilted and stuffy. When he received the invitation to speak at their monthly meeting, he wasn't sure how to take it. He had called the representative to check if it was him they really wanted; and if so why. The response was unequivocal. 'Ah yes, absolutely; we've heard a lot about what's going on at Baines Electronics and one of our committee members suggested that you would be the person to tell us about it.'

He didn't see himself as a public speaker. He asked Evelyn if she would go. 'It's you they've invited,' she told him. 'Just tell your story.'

He spoke with Stella; after all, she had taken on the role of heading up the programme now. 'No,' she said emphatically. 'You're the one who started us on this whole thing. Besides, it's time somebody acknowledged you for that.'

So it was that he stood at the lectern, poised with his PowerPoint presentation, telling an audience of business people about E-Fitness coaching and how it was transforming his company.

'We don't talk about this much,' he told them. 'We don't take a look at how employees feel about working for us, or what makes them want to continue with us, or why so many people seem to succumb to stress. We don't face the fact that absenteeism, high staff turnover, inadequate productivity, wastage and mediocre customer relations account for costs that just about equal our profit margins. That means we could double our profits.' He looked around the room. 'Or make one,' he added. It was the first time that he heard some laughter and began to warm to his topic.

He gave them the statistics: how Baines Electronics had increased its revenue, lowered its costs and grown its business. This caught their attention. When he talked about individual stories of personal success, or how a team had developed a brand new idea that had been utilized throughout the company, the audience looked rapt. When he spoke about some of the E-Fitness coaching, he noticed a little restlessness and wondered if it was because of the time or that they didn't really want to do anything.

At the end of the evening, he sensed a certain politeness in the thanks he received and a reserve among the audience, few of whom came over to talk with him.

It wasn't until a week or two later that the calls started to come in.

The ripple effect

Congratulations. Having arrived at this point means that you have accompanied Adam and the others on a journey that you could now be willing to take for yourself. You are ready for it once you have tried and fully experienced each of the tools described in this book.

Be aware of this: the processes, or tools, are powerful and empowering, and they affect not only the person going through them.

Once your understanding, your outlook and your behaviour change, others are influenced by them. Throw that stone into a pond and watch the ripples flow outwards. Nothing can stop them. Coach one person using these methods and you will be touching 10. Give one person the tools so that they coach others and you will have had an effect on hundreds, if not thousands, most of whom you will never meet.

Exercise

Who will you talk to about this? Make a list of at least 10 people, and then make arrangements to see them. And don't forget to have fun.

REFERENCES

Books

Bar-On, Reuven *EQ-i Leadership User's Guide*, Multi-Health Systems (2006)

Berne, Eric *Games People Play*, Grove Press (1964)

Cleese, John (video) *Meetings, Bloody Meetings*, Video Arts

Cleese, John (video) *The Helping Hand*, Video Arts

Covey, Stephen *The 7 Habits of Highly Effective People*, Simon & Schuster (1997)

Goleman, Daniel *Emotional Intelligence*, Random House (1996)

Goleman, Daniel *Working with Emotional Intelligence*, Bantam (1998)

Harris, Thomas *I'm OK, You're OK*, Avon Books (1973)

Heimler, Eugene *Survival in Society*, Weidenfeld and Nicolson (1975)

Heimler, Eugene *The Healing Echo*, Souvenir Press (1985)

Hidden, Anthony (Hidden Report) *Investigation into the Clapham Junction Railway Accident* (1989)

Layton, Jack *Last Letter to Canadians* (2011)

Maté, Gabor *When the Body Says No, understanding the stress–disease connection*, John Wiley (2003)

Nin, Anaïs *The Diary of Anaïs Nin 1931–34*, Harcourt (1994)

Perls, Frederick (Fritz) *Gestalt Therapy Verbatim*, Real People Press (1969)

Pink, Daniel *A Whole New Mind*, Riverhead Books (2005)

Redman, Warren *Portfolios for Development*, Kogan Page (1994)

Redman, Warren *Achieving Personal Success*, Merlin Star Press (1996)

Redman, Warren *The 9 Steps to Emotional Fitness*, Merlin Star Press (2003)

Redman, Warren *Recipes for Inner Peace*, Merlin Star Press (2005)

Rogers, Carl *On Becoming a Person*, Houghton Mifflin (1961)

Rogers, William (Rogers Commission) *Report of the presidential commission on the Space Shuttle Challenger Accident* (1986)

Sun Tzu *The Art of War*, Simon and Brown (2011)

Organizational references

British Association of Counselling and Psychotherapy (BACP) Coaching section: **http://www.bacpcoaching.co.uk/**

Emotional Fitness Institute: **http://www.EFitInstitute.com**

International Coach Federation (ICF) Ethics: **http://www.coachfederation.org/ethics/**

INDEX